D0484630

CULTURE SMART!

BOSNIA AND
HERZEGOVINA

Elizabeth Hammond

·K·U·P·E·R·A·R·D·

First published in Great Britain 2009
by Kuperard, an imprint of Bravo Ltd
59 Hutton Grove, London N12 8DS
Tel: +44 (0) 20 8446 2440   Fax: +44 (0) 20 8446 2441
www.culturesmartguides.com
Inquiries: sales@kuperard.co.uk

Culture Smart! is a registered trademark of Bravo Ltd

Distributed in the United States and Canada
by Random House Distribution Services
1745 Broadway, New York, NY 10019
Tel: +1 (212) 572-2844   Fax: +1 (212) 572-4961
Inquiries: csorders@randomhouse.com

Series Editor Geoffrey Chesler
Design Bobby Birchall

ISBN 978 1 85733 484 5

British Library Cataloguing in Publication Data
A CIP catalogue entry for this book is available from the
British Library

Printed in Malaysia

Cover image: Sixteenth-century bridge over the Neretva River, Mostar.
© Stefan Andronache/Fotolia.com

The photographs on pages 43, 57, 75, 116, 121, and 163 are reproduced by
permission of the author; the photo on page 40 (left) by permission of Melinda Walton.

Pages 73 © Zoransimin/Dreamstime.com; 83 © Sote 2/Dreamstime.com

Images on the following pages reproduced under Creative Commons License
Attribution 2.5: 13 (top) © Hieronim Woźniak; 13 (bottom) © Robert Scoble;
15 © Zoran Pravdić; 17, 18, 101, 102, 103, 104, 115, 117 © D J Bungi;
19 © Ramirez HUN; 38, 40 (right) © Mikhail Evstafiev; 44 © BloodSaric; 51, 53
(bottom), 111 © Christian Bickel; 53 (top) © Ante Perkovic; 76 © SpeedyGonsales;
90 © johovac; 91 © Modzzak; 101 (top) © Filip Knežić; 105 (top) © Matěj Baťha;
113 © M+7; 115 (bottom) © Daniel Aragay; 123 © Martin Belam;
131, 134 © Mazbin; and 164 © Josep Renalias.

About the Author

ELIZABETH HAMMOND has a degree in English and Clinical Psychology from Tufts University and a master's in International Health from The Johns Hopkins School of Public Health. While a professor at the University of Sarajevo on a Fulbright scholarship, she also taught at the University of Zenica and the Sarajevo Medresa. Over the course of multiple visits to the region, she studied the long-term psychological effects of the war in Bosnia and the development of the country's health care system. Her research was presented at the Institute for Global Studies at Tufts University and at The Johns Hopkins School of Public Health.

The Culture Smart! series is continuing to expand.
For further information and latest titles visit
www.culturesmartguides.com

The publishers would like to thank **CultureSmart!**Consulting for its help in researching and developing the concept for this series.

CultureSmart!Consulting creates tailor-made seminars and consultancy programs to meet a wide range of corporate, public-sector, and individual needs. Whether delivering courses on multicultural team building in the USA, preparing Chinese engineers for a posting in Europe, training call-center staff in India, or raising the awareness of police forces to the needs of diverse ethnic communities, it provides essential, practical, and powerful skills worldwide to an increasingly international workforce.

For details, visit www.culturesmartconsulting.com

CultureSmart!Consulting and **CultureSmart!** guides have both contributed to and featured regularly in the weekly travel program "Fast Track" on BBC World TV.

contents

contents

Map of Bosnia and Herzegovina

introduction

Bosnia and Herzegovina is a country of contradictions, where East meets West, and where several ideologies have come together to evolve into a vibrant, diverse culture. While there may be much that the Western visitor will find familiar in the day-to-day life here, there are differences that can be startling.

Bosnia is a unique combination of religious values, communist secularism, Western attitudes, and Eastern practices. The people are warm, open, and eager to move forward—but are hampered by their memories of a conflict-filled past. The breathtaking landscape varies widely across the country—but pollution is an increasing problem. The economic situation is improving—but capitalism hasn't fully taken hold. The people espouse Western attitudes—but remain family-centered and uphold traditional gender roles. In sum, nothing can be taken for granted.

The trauma of recent history remains palpable, evidenced both by the bullet holes visible in city buildings and by a somewhat downtrodden attitude that can unexpectedly rise to the surface in your Bosnian friends and colleagues. After the devastating effects of the war in the 1990s, Bosnians today have a renewed appreciation for family and a widespread distrust of government.

Bosnia is a beautifully complex country, but it is a country at a crossroads. With its dramatic history and uncertain future, it is unlike any other part of Europe. The culture can be confusing, and the bureaucracy frustrating, even to the locals. To feel really comfortable here, it's best to adopt the local attitude of "what will be, will be," with shoulders shrugged and arms raised to the sky.

Culture Smart! Bosnia will help you to understand the quirks of Bosnian society and introduce you to a friendly, hospitable people who are proud of their history but pessimistic about their future. Armed with the knowledge it provides, you will be able to operate successfully in Bosnian business and social spheres alike.

The early chapters give a general overview of the history and customs of the land, and the way of life of the people. Later you will find tips on etiquette and social situations, and suggestions for dealing with specific circumstances, such as how to get prompt service in a restaurant, or how to tell a cabdriver to get you to your meeting on time. You will find out how to make contact and establish lifelong relationships with the locals— and how they drink their coffee.

Despite the violence in its past, Bosnia has a great deal to offer its guests today. The well-informed visitor, armed with knowledge about the cultural context behind the dos and don'ts, will be rewarded with new friends, warm hospitality, and a deeper understanding of this fascinating land.

Key Facts

Official Name	Bosna-Hercegovina (Bosnia and Herzegovina)	Declared independence in March 1992
Capital City	Sarajevo Pop. 380,000	
Other Major Cities	Banja Luka, Mostar, Zenica, Travnik, Tuzla, Bihać	The country is divided into two political entities: the Republika Srpska and the Federation.
Area	19,741 sq. miles (51,129 sq. km). Nearly landlocked; short coastline on Adriatic Sea	
Borders	Croatia, Serbia, Montenegro	
Climate	Cold winters with heavy precipitation; warm summers	Conditions can vary widely across the country owing to the differences in terrain, including mountains, plains, valleys, and coastline
Currency	Bosnian Convertible Mark (BAM, or KM)	Pegged to the Euro at 2:1
Population	4,590,310 (est. 2008)	
Ethnic Makeup	Bosniak (40%), Serb (37%), Croat (14%)	
Language	Bosnian-Croatian-Serbian. Uses Latin script in the Federation and Cyrillic in the Republika Srpska	

Religion	Muslim (40%), Eastern Orthodox (31%), Roman Catholic (15%), other (14%)	
Government	Federal Demographic Republic. Bicameral parliament at federal level. Power is shared between three presidents. At local level the Federation and the RS have regional parliaments.	The Federation is made up of ten regional cantons. The RS relies on municipal governments for local concerns.
Media	The public broadcasting system, JRTS BiH, includes three legal entities: RTFBiH, BHRT, and RTRS, which together provide state-wide TV and radio channels.	Local daily newspapers: *Oslobodjenje, Dnevni Avaz, Dnevni List, Nezavisne Novine.* Popular magazines: *Dani, Slobodna Bosna, Start, Most*
Media: Foreign Language	Satellite and cable TV available with some English channels	
Electricity	220 volts, 50 Hz	Two-pronged plugs; US devices require an adapter.
Video/TV	PAL B/H	
Telephone	Country code: 387	To call abroad, dial 00 followed by the country code.
Internet Domain	.ba	
Time Zone	Central European Time: GMT +1	

chapter one

LAND & PEOPLE

Most people remember Bosnia as a place they saw on the news in the 1990s. The reality of modern-day Bosnia is quite different, but still remains irrevocably tied to the recent past. The cautious traveler can relax—yes, there is electricity here, as well as plenty of cable TV, flushing toilets, and a literate, educated populace. True, the standard of living is not what it is in other parts of Europe, but Bosnia is anything but medieval.

That said, Bosnia remains behind Europe in terms of its political and economic development. Despite the widespread secularization and modernization that occurred in the mid-twentieth century, some of this was reversed in the recent

conflict. In addition, the issues raised by war fifteen years past have stymied progress today.

The last census was conducted in 1990. The three main ethnic groups in the country—the Serbs, the Croats, and the Bosniaks (Bosnian Muslims)—were fairly evenly distributed across Bosnia, which was then part of Yugoslavia. The next census is likely to take place in 2011, and promises to be provocative, illustrating the dramatic shifts in demography that have occurred in the last twenty years. As a result of ethnic cleansing in the 1990s, the northern parts of Bosnia are now mainly Serb. Sarajevo is a great deal more Muslim than it was in 1990, and Croats continue to dominate in the west.

The three main ethnic groups were defined in the early twentieth century, when Serbia and Croatia made bids for land. Using nationalist

rhetoric, Croatians defined Bosnian Catholics as Croats, and Serbs defined Bosnian Orthodox as Serbs. Note that although religion is a major factor in the definition of these groups, it is not absolute—not all Muslims consider themselves to be Bosniaks, for example. These labels persist today, and are a defining factor within the Bosnian population. After the war, the groups became even more homogeneous.

Today, the country is roughly 40 percent Bosniak, 37 percent Serb, and 14 percent Croat. In some areas of the country, especially in the rural parts, these groups may exist in homogeneous pockets. In the cities, groups of friends may consist of individuals from all groups and intermarriage is barely noticed in the more progressive circles. Regardless, all Bosnians come from a common history of coexistence, tolerance, and open-mindedness, and most Bosnians demonstrate goodwill and tolerance toward other groups. However, in terms of politics, religion, and one's immediate social group, ethnic lines are still a major factor. For hundreds of years, cultures and religions mingled in the streets of Sarajevo—sometimes harmoniously, sometimes less so. The end result is a land of fascinating contradictions and a unique people.

GEOGRAPHICAL OVERVIEW

One of Bosnia's most valuable natural resources is the land and scenery of the country. It is full of

mountains and valleys, lakes and rivers, wide plains, and even has a shoreline of nearly twelve and a half miles (20 km). Ecotourism is a popular new buzzword, although little is currently being done to preserve the natural beauty of the land.

Bosnia is bordered by Croatia to the west and north, by Serbia to the east, and by Montenegro to the south. It interrupts the Croatian coastline at the town of Neum, gaining a few miles of ocean access. Called the "heart-shaped land" by locals, it is a place where East meets West, and where traditional values meld with modern aspirations.

Covering 19,741 square miles (51,129 sq. km), Bosnia is about the size of West Virginia, or of England. The 1990 census set the population at around four million; current estimates mark it slightly higher, at 4,590,310. There is a widely scattered diaspora across Europe, North America, and Australia.

Bosnia is divided into a number of regions that were created at the end of the war. Two entities, the

Republika Srpska (RS) and the Federation, form the main boundaries. Herzegovina, to the south and west, is not recognized as a politically separate region, but is an important distinction. It is similar to the Croatian climate and landscape, with scraggly hills surrounding vineyards and orange groves that stretch across long plains in the valleys between.

To the north, in the Republika Srpska, the landscape is defined by clean, rushing rivers and forested mountains. In the northeast, broad plains make the region one of the most fertile agricultural areas in the country. Central Bosnia is mountainous and hilly, with many mineral resources, including silver, gold, copper, salt, and coal. This is the heart of industrial Bosnia. Much of Bosnia is covered by freshwater lakes, rivers, and streams, and mineral water is a big export. Sadly, environmental awareness has not yet reached the policy level. Air pollution from the industrial plants, a lax attitude toward littering, and uncontrolled use of natural resources put one of Bosnia's greatest treasures at risk.

When referring to the country, it is politically correct to use its full name: Bosnia and Herzegovina. For the sake of convenience, it is commonly called simply Bosnia or BiH. The Republika Srpska is commonly referred to as the RS. These forms will be used throughout this book.

CLIMATE

This small country's broad range of geographical features means that the climate can vary greatly from place to place. The seasons are predictable, however, and dramatic storms are rare, although there are occasional mild earthquakes.

The Dinaric Alps traverse the country diagonally, descending from the northwest, through the heart of the country, and into Montenegro. This mountain chain separates Herzegovina from the rest of Bosnia, providing sharp relief between the Mediterranean climate of Herzegovina and the harsher climates of central Bosnia. Temperatures and weather change dramatically as one moves west, making Herzegovina a welcome respite from the cold winters, and an ideal situation for its numerous vineyards and citrus groves.

Herzegovina is more temperate than the rest of Bosnia, and is more consistently sunny and dry, even in winter. In other parts of the country, the summers are hot, the winters are cold with substantial snowfall, and spring and fall are brief, cool, and rainy. Typically, cooler weather sets in during October and can last throughout May and even into June. It snows frequently, though Bosnians will be quick to tell you that global warming is responsible for the poor ski conditions on any particular day. In general, the winters are gloomy and gray, and most people stay indoors, making even bustling Sarajevo seem quiet. Average temperatures in central Bosnia (including Sarajevo) range from about 20°–35°F (-6°–1°C) in winter, and 75°–85°F (24°–30°C) in summer.

The country comes alive in the summer months. Cafés spill on to the streets and sidewalks, dress becomes a great deal less conservative, and the cities hum with activity. Summer is an ideal time to visit. There are no crowds—just sunshine.

CITY LIFE

The hub of the country is the capital, Sarajevo, a city with a rich history, a confluence of modern and traditional ideas, and literally at the border of the

East-dominated RS and the Western-looking Federation. Sarajevo hosts a variety of ethnicities in a population of around 400,000— about the size of Boston proper.

Banja Luka is the second-largest city in Bosnia, and the capital of the RS. It has a mainly Serb population of about 200,000. It is a vibrant city, with an upbeat attitude and a thriving nightlife.

The urban center of Herzegovina is Mostar, with about 100,000 residents. This beautiful city is still torn by ethnic divisions, with Muslims living on the east bank and Croats on the west. The city remains divided, with separate government and school systems for the two groups.

Tuzla and Zenica are industrial towns with larger populations in central Bosnia. Zenica is about an hour from Sarajevo with around 120,000 residents. Tuzla, in the northeastern part of the Federation, has around 170,000 people.

Travnik, a smaller city, boasts a number of cultural attractions that make it a popular place to visit, including a fourteenth-century medieval fortress. Bihać, in the northwestern corner of the RS, a charming little town on the clear, cold banks of the Una River, is a popular rafting destination.

A BRIEF HISTORY

For centuries, Bosnia has sat at the cusp of East and West, making it a natural battleground for ideologies and empires alike. In the past its people retreated for safety into the mountains or were swept into whatever the ruling power of the time might be; modern Bosnia has no such refuge or overarching ruling power. Desirous of change, capable of progress, many Bosnians nonetheless remain pessimistic about their immediate future.

The recent war in BiH is commonly attributed to centuries-old ethnic divisions; modern scholarship shows that this is an inaccurate and dangerous idea used by political leaders to justify the conflict as an inevitable consequence of historical circumstances. It is true that Bosnia has had more than its fair share of conflict in the last five hundred years, but the modern tensions are not causally related to such events, or not directly. Bosnian Croats do not necessarily come from Croatia, and Bosnian Serbs are not necessarily from Serbia; rather, these identifying titles were applied in the early twentieth century as Croatia and Serbia vied for territory. As any Bosnian will proudly tell you, before the war they lived quite peacefully with neighbors of all ethnicities. To be fair, this isn't completely true either. There were periods of intergroup conflict and periods of intergroup peace; examples of either are often used to make political points. The important thing to understand is that Bosnia's history is not a fatalistic one, but it has been used in incendiary ways. Some scholars and politicians today still use fragments of Bosnian history to redefine the present in convenient ways, either by claiming land or power for certain ethnic groups, or to incite fear. Bosnia's history did not determine the recent war, but it does help to explain some of the political tactics used by the main participants.

The story of Bosnia is complex and utterly riveting. Its history is full of kings, brave heroes, tragic losses, and brilliant victories. The rich resources of the area, combined with its position between the Austro–Hungarian Empire and the Ottoman Empire, always made Bosnia a desirable prize. Trade routes through the region have existed for as long as records show. An original "melting pot" of Europe, Bosnia reflects the convergence of many peoples and ideologies.

People have inhabited the region since prehistoric times, and there is evidence of a Neanderthal presence dating to the mid-Paleolithic age. Examination of the archaeological history has started, and the National Museum in Sarajevo and smaller museums throughout the country include collections of ancient pottery and metalwork that are thousands of years old. Subsequent visitors from many lands have settled the region. A look at Bosnia's history shows the great variety of influences that have molded the culture of the modern country.

The Roman Empire

Balkan culture can be traced back to the Indo-European Illyrian tribes who inhabited the area during the Iron Age. These include the Delmatae, who raised animals; the Illyrian–Celtic Scordisci tribe; and the Daesitates, a warlike group, who were the last to fall under Roman control. The Romans attacked the tribes in the area of today's Croatia in the third century BCE, and established a stronghold there. As they moved inland they encountered greater resistance from the inhabitants, who were brave and fierce, and massive numbers of Roman troops were needed to overcome them. Octavian, soon to become the Emperor Augustus, finally conquered the area around 33 BCE. The battles of this era are legendary, and stories of the determination and ferocity of the ancient Illyrians are told even today.

The Illyrian clans were absorbed into the Roman Empire, and the Romans quickly established provinces in the region; modern-day Bosnia fell within the provinces of Dalmatia and Pannonia. Roman soldiers were encouraged to settle in the region and Roman culture permeated the Balkans, heralding the introduction of the Latin alphabet and Christianity. However, traditional beliefs persisted in the more isolated areas. On the division of the Roman Empire into two in 395 CE, Bosnia stayed in the west, along with modern-day Croatia and Slovenia, while Serbia to the east became part of the Byzantine Empire.

The Slavic Settlement

The Western Roman Empire dissolved in the fifth century, and various groups attacked the region over the next few centuries, including the Goths, the Asiatic Huns, the Iranian Alans, the Turkish Avars, and, most importantly, the Slavs. The Slavs became the dominant group sometime after the sixth century, and established agricultural colonies throughout the entire Balkan region. They integrated into Bosnian culture over the next several centuries, creating a uniquely diverse ethnic group with pagan, Roman, Hellenistic, Celtic, and Slavic elements.

The influence of the Slavs and the fall of the Roman Empire in the west brought Bosnia into the orbit of the Byzantine Empire. Now there was

pressure from both the Latin West and the Orthodox East to turn Bosnia into a Christian land, and Orthodox and Catholic forces continued to vie for influence into the Middle Ages. The Slavs in Bosnia resisted adopting either, preferring a specific form of Christianity developed by Slavic missionaries in the ninth century. In defiance of external influence, Bosnians created the Bosnian Church. The Pope responded by declaring all its members to be heretics, giving Hungary the justification to try to take Bosnia by force.

An Independent Bosnia

From the twelfth to the fifteenth centuries, the Bosnians lived largely without foreign control, although they were experiencing heavy pressure from their Hungarian neighbors. One of the heroes of Bosnian history during this time is Ban Kulin, whose reign from 1180 to 1204 was marked by peace and expanding economic stability. He opened trade routes to the Dalmatian coast and took advantage of the rich mineral resources of central Bosnia. He managed the threats from Rome and Hungary with astute diplomacy, and ballads about the legendary Ban Kulin are still sung today.

Ban Kulin's efforts were not enough to staunch the flow of Hungarian troops into Bosnia, however. Hungary effectively controlled Croatia, and was pressing for control of the region. The Roman Catholic Church reluctantly agreed to its quest for dominance on the condition that it would eliminate heresy from the Bosnian Church, and, for a while, Bosnia was under Hungarian control.

The Hungarians retreated in 1241 to rebuff an encroaching Mongol threat, and new Bosnian heroes emerged. Ban Stephen Kotromanić II ruled from 1322 to 1353, and was responsible for uniting various Bosnian territories, including modern Herzegovina, and for developing the economic potential of the region. He actively negotiated with the surrounding countries, helping to put Bosnia on the European map. Nonetheless, his support of the Bosnian Church put him in uncertain standing with Rome. To counter this, he allowed the establishment of Franciscan monasteries in 1340. This led the way for the Catholicization of BiH and greatly influenced the later development of the state.

Kotromanić's successor, his nephew Stephen Tvrtko I, ascended the throne at only fifteen years of age in the mid-fourteenth century. With the help of the Hungarian king, he managed to make Bosnia the most powerful state in the Balkans. He expanded the region so much that he assumed the title "King of Croatia, Dalmatia, and Bosnia."

Bosnia's early history was marked by expansion, growing political and economic importance, and strong leadership within the country. Despite this beginning, things were about to change.

Ottoman Rule (1463–1878)

After Tvrtko's death, Bosnia lacked strong leadership and lost much of the territory it had gained. At the start of the fifteenth century, two rival groups fought to control the region: King Ostoja, supported by Hungary, and Tvrtko II, supported by the Ottomans. They frequently traded power, one constantly overthrowing the other. Alliances were continually shifting and rivalry was intense. The discord eventually resulted in the establishment of Ottoman rule.

When Tvrtko II died, Stephen Tomaš took control in 1443. In desperation from increasing Ottoman attacks, Tomaš caved in to papal pressure and eliminated the Bosnian Church in exchange for support from Rome.

The support from Rome was not enough to protect Bosnia from the Ottomans, however, and the Bosnian state fell to Turkish forces in 1528 under Tomaš's successor, Stephen Tomašević.

The Turks were motivated by economic gain rather than ideological goals, as Rome was, and they sought control over Bosnia in order to widen their tax base and increase access to potential army recruits. Bosnia also provided a jumping-off point for military campaigns into Austro–Hungarian territory. This specific motivation would have a great impact on the development of the country while under Turkish rule over the next four centuries.

For example, there was little about Turkish rule that inhibited the free practice of religion. While Muslims were granted some advantages, Christians, especially Orthodox Christians, could still move up the ranks in the government or military without converting. On the other hand, as long as new conscripts and riches flowed into the

Ottoman Empire, there was little concern with how local officials behaved, and abuses by the local *pashas* (governors) had more of an effect on the local population than the laws of the Empire as a whole. Essentially, the Turks cared little for the religion or habits of the Bosnian people, as long as the money and troops continued to flow into the Empire.

During the early Ottoman presence in the Balkans, young men and boys were taken from their families for training in Istanbul to work as servants in the sultan's retinue or as administrative officials. These janissary troops were fundamental to the functioning of the Empire, and it is estimated that around 200,000 Balkan boys were recruited during the fifteenth and sixteenth centuries. The system was brutal, but generally popular with the local population, as it afforded the boys the opportunity to be educated and potentially achieve a position of status.

As Turkish power solidified over the region, conversions to Islam increased and an exodus of Catholics into Austria–Hungary resulted in a pretty even mix of Muslims and Christians in Bosnia at the beginning of the sixteenth century. The Orthodox Church actually grew under Ottoman rule, as it was a more accepted form of Christianity than Catholicism, the religion of the enemy Austro–Hungarians.

The Sarajevo Haggadah

Bosnia's small community of Sephardic Jews settled in the country during the Ottoman period, after being expelled from Spain and Portugal in 1492 and 1497. They were widely tolerated and allowed to practice their religion openly. The Jewish population in Bosnia dropped from 14,000 to 4,000 during the course of the Second World War, and only a few remain today. One of Bosnia's great historical artifacts is an antique illuminated *Haggadah,* the Jewish religious text used during the Passover supper, which is on view at the National Museum in Sarajevo.

The influence of the Ottomans on Bosnia was immense, and is still strongly visible. Most of today's towns, cities, roads, and bridges were built under the centralized urbanization plans of the Ottomans. In addition, there was substantial intellectual, religious, artistic, and cultural growth during this period.

The story of the decline of the Ottoman Empire and the rise of the Austro–Hungarian Empire is bloody, sporadic, and full of victories for both sides. The Ottomans began to lose their hold in the 1680s, and when Eugene of Savoy torched Sarajevo in 1697, many Catholics fled with him, fearing reprisals. The Turks increased taxes in an effort to raise funds against the encroaching Austro–Hungarian army, which only led to tax revolts in the eighteenth century. Coupled with 20,000 deaths as a result of the plague in the 1730s, Turkish rule was seriously threatened.

Meanwhile, bloody revolts in Serbia forced the Turks to grant increasing autonomy to the Balkan territories. There were widespread tax revolts and general discontent with Turkish rule. Bosnian governors seized the political opportunity, offering military assistance to the Turks in return for tax waivers and guaranteed self-rule. In this way, Bosnia dramatically shifted away from direct Turkish rule. The Turks, fighting battles on all sides, could not maintain control of the territory. In a final blow to Turkish rule, Russia declared war on the Ottoman Empire in 1877, amid a wide-scale rebellion in the Balkans from 1875 to '78.

Austrian Protectorate (1878–1918)
Starting with the Congress of Berlin in 1878, the Austro–Hungarians wasted no time in asserting their control over the Balkans. They were eager

to exploit the natural resources of the region and to build a buffer between themselves and Russia, with hopes of expanding into the east. A policy of Europeanization was implemented, and European styles of dress, cuisine, architecture, and manners were everywhere. At the same time, Bosnian infrastructure and industries were developed and streamlined, and new modes of industry existed alongside a feudal system that dominated the agricultural industries.

Centuries of occupation, however, made Bosnians unwilling to accept a new ruling power without a fight. The period of occupation and annexation by Austria–Hungary was full of rebellions of increasing sophistication. The influx of European ideas not only expanded Bosnian industry, but also alerted its citizens to their exploitation and gave them the tools to resist it. The development of infrastructure—roads, a railway, mining, and metallurgy—led to a new urban working class, who began to outnumber peasants, hitherto the majority of Bosnians. The flow of European ideas also led to modern forms of industry, resulting in workers' unions and organized strikes.

With little faith in the local populace, foreign officials governed the state with a heavy hand. Benjamin Kallay, the Austro–Hungarian administrator of Bosnia–Herzegovina for more than two decades, recognized the unrest that characterized the region. Bosnia had almost no history or experience with self-governance, and Kallay exploited this fact by trying to create divisions between the people. He deflected the Bosnian fervor for independence by playing up transnational identities, such as Orthodox, Catholic, or Muslim. This was initially successful, and defined much of the century to follow, but the flood of revolutionary ideas could not be stopped. Nationalist rebellions erupted in addition to class rebellions.

It was a period of rapid social change and great unrest. As new ideas poured into the region, Bosnians responded with a wave of local publications that only fanned the flames of a social discontent that was becoming increasingly difficult for the Austro–Hungarians to manage. In an attempt to bring the area under tighter control, BiH was officially annexed in 1908. This was not well received by Bosnians, and Serbs in particular. In a definitive act of defiance, a Serb nationalist, Gavrilo Princip, shot the Archduke Franz Ferdinand and his pregnant wife on June 28, 1914. It was the end of Austro–Hungarian rule and the start of the First World War.

The Kingdom of Serbs, Croats, and Slovenes (1918–41)

A comprehensive account of the First World War and Bosnia's involvement would deserve a book in itself, but essentially, several empires used

tensions in the Balkans for
their own purposes. There
was no real relief of these
tensions with the end of the
First World War, except for
the removal of Habsburg
control over the Balkan
region. The resulting

formation of the Kingdom of Serbs, Croats, and
Slovenes was an uneasy alliance of groups with
very different ideas on how to run a country.
During this unsettled time, serfdom was
abolished in Bosnia and massive land reforms
reassigned property to the peasants.

The Kingdom was renamed "Yugoslavia" by
King Alexander in 1929, but this did not lead to
peace. Serbia continued to push for a centralized
state, while Croatia desired more independence
and local control. Bosnia was caught in the
middle. While the various political parties fought
over the shape their country should take, Hitler
was gaining influence in the region. The Croatian
national socialist/fascist Ustaše movement was
founded by one of Hitler's and Mussolini's
admirers, Ante Pavelić, in the 1930s. Based in
Italy until the beginning of the Second World
War, Pavelić helped to establish the puppet
Ustaše regime in Croatia that would turn
Yugoslavia into a battleground for the Axis and
Allied troops. Until this point, Yugoslavia had
maintained a policy of appeasement toward
Hitler, but Germany invaded the country on

April 6, 1941. After eleven days of resistance, Yugoslavia surrendered. In return for Ustaše support, the Axis powers created "The Independent State of Croatia" (or NDH), which included Bosnia. This did not sit well with Serbs and Muslims and civil war ensued.

Occupation and Resistance (1941–45)
The Ustaše regime sought to eliminate Serb resistance through ethnic cleansing and widespread atrocities. Četniks—Serbs who favored the reestablishment of the monarchy—banded together to resist the Croats in the hope that, with enough recruitment and long-term resistance, they would be able  to reestablish a Serbian state after the Germans were defeated.

Pro-Nazi rule led to widespread persecution of Jewish, Serbian, and Gypsy civilians. Croatian supporters of Hitler instituted anti-Jewish laws almost immediately, and most of the Jews in BiH were sent to concentration camps.

Amid the nationalist aims of the Četniks and the independence movement of the German-allied Croats, a small party of Stalinist-style Communists, led by Josip Broz Tito, envisioned a social revolution to replace either a Croatian or a Serbian state. Many people were tired of nationalist agendas and saw Communism as an opportunity for peace.

Tito proved to be a military hero as well as a political icon. He first drew attention during the First World War, but his cunning and his strategic genius were widely recognized during the Second. The Communist partisans would, however, face heavy losses before the war was over.

In late 1943 and '44, the partisans gained the support of Allied forces. In November 1943, the second session of the Anti-Fascist Council of National Liberation of Yugoslavia (AVNOJ) declared BiH a multiethnic Communist state. Tito continued to attract former Ustaše supporters, who were becoming increasingly disaffected as Soviet troops gained control over more of the region. A new era began.

The Socialist Federal Republic of Yugoslavia (1945–90)
Bosnia became one of the six constituent republics in socialist Yugoslavia led by Tito. To most Westerners, trained to fear Communism after the Cold War, Tito was a dangerous tyrant. Many Bosnians tell a different story, however. The story

of Tito's time in power is complicated, for he indisputably united the country and promoted economic stability and intellectual growth. At the same time, more than 250,000 Croats, Muslims, and Serbs were killed as Tito's regime rooted out nationalist sympathizers (or those suspected of being such), and religious practice was severely limited in public.

Led by the Department for the Protection of the People, Tito's secret police, former Ustaše members (mostly Croats), the Franciscan clergy, Četniks, and Muslims received especially harsh punishments. Muslim women were forbidden to wear the veil, Islamic courts were outlawed, and Islamic education for children was banned.

Tito spent the 1950s establishing power, fostering a sense of nationalism for the country, and weeding out opposition. He later liberalized his policies after Stalin expelled him from the Cominform, a Soviet-led group of Communist parties. For example, religious practice became tolerated under state direction and religious persecution lessened. By the 1960s, the party focused on rebuilding the state. Many Bosnians proudly remember this era as a time when everyone had a job. Using both Russian and American money, he built roads, schools, libraries, and medical facilities.

Things began to change in the 1970s, when Croat and Serbian nationalist movements began to resurface. Tito's government was based in Belgrade and dominated by Serb officials. Many of the regions under Tito's control were contentiously fought over by Serb or Croatian nationalists. These sentiments would fuel the fire of the 1990s conflict.

Tito died in 1980. Without his strong leadership, Bosnia began to deteriorate economically as the decade progressed. Slobodan Milošević gained power among the Serbian Communists during this time, and maintained popularity among Serbs through a strongly nationalist set of policies. He revoked the autonomy of Kosovo and Vojvodina, causing massive protests from those who lived there.

After the fall of the Berlin Wall and the dissolution of the Soviet Union, some of the Yugoslav republics, namely Croatia and Slovenia, started pushing for more independence. Croatian nationalism was growing ever more radical in competition with Milošević's increasingly brazen calls for a Greater Serbia. A turning point occurred in 1989 at Kosovo Polje, a town that held special significance for Serbs as the site of a battle and the death of a Serb hero, Prince Lazar, in 1389. During a speech there, Milošević openly referred to armed conflict as potentially being necessary to resolve the current crisis.

Neighboring Croatia was split between a nationalist party led by Franjo Tuđman (the HDZ) and a Serb-led party, the Serbian Democratic Party (SDS). Many Serbs feared the reestablishment of the Ustaše state, and Serb media machines took advantage of Tuđman's nationalist rhetoric to stir up opposition. The Serbs utilized many techniques to create distrust. They were known to stage violent encounters between Serbs and Muslims, thereby scaring the local populations into taking up arms. They then cited the violence as an excuse to move in the Serbian army.

In 1991, the Serb–Croat civil war spread disorder into Bosnia, and Bosnia was once again caught in the middle. The HDZ was active in Bosnia, as was the SDS, led by Radovan Karadžić. Alija Izetbegović led the third major party, the Muslim Party of Democratic Action (SDA). Izetbegović's party won the majority of votes in the 1990 election, so he was effectively the leader of the country, but the ethnic lines within the political paties resulted in a disjointed and divided government. Muslims made

up nearly half the population of Bosnia before the war, and had become widely secular under Tito's regime. Nonetheless, the SDS focused its media campaign on the threat of Islamic fundamentalism. In the meantime, the Serbian army began quietly occupying small villages in BiH, surrounding Sarajevo and other cities.

The War in Bosnia (1992–95)

Bosnia and Herzegovina declared independence from Yugoslavia in March 1992 after a referendum that was widely supported by Muslims and Croats, but boycotted by Serbs. The EU and the UN quickly recognized Bosnia's independence; later that day, Serb forces attacked Sarajevo. Sarajevo's citizens poured into the streets in a peaceful protest while Serb snipers fired into the crowd.

As the rest of the world stood dumbfounded, Serb forces pushed across northern Bosnia. As they

went, they systematically killed or displaced all non-Serbs from the area with frightening effectiveness. At the same time they used scare tactics to frighten Bosnian Serbs, mostly peasants, about Croatian nationalism and supposed Muslim *jihad*. As many still remembered the great number of Serbs killed under the Croatian Ustaše movement, this was not a hard sell.

The Serb army (JNA) also used systematic genocidal tactics to secure their dream of a Greater Serbia. Mass rapes and killings, such as in concentration camps, took place in northern Bosnia.

The war in Yugoslavia was not like other wars to date. Despite recognizing the sovereignty of an

independent Bosnia–Herzegovina, the
international community persisted in calling
it a civil war, severely limiting the kind of
interventions that could take place. In the wake
of the failures of intervention in Somalia and
Rwanda, many were nervous about getting
involved. The UN sent peacekeepers to Bosnia,
but they did not have the right to fire their
weapons. The mission was called UNPROFOR,
and was almost entirely ineffective due to the
constraints of international law that mandated
its neutrality. Serb guns made no distinctions
between peacekeepers and civilians, and
peacekeepers were, by law, instructed to do no
more than watch as civilians were massacred.

One of the most outrageous instances of this
policy was the massacre at Srebrenica in 1995. Serb
troops rounded up 7,000 men and boys and shot
them in the fields around this small mountain town.
Entire families were wiped out in a single day, and
the area has not recovered from this epic tragedy.

At the start of the conflict, the JNA was the fourth-largest standing army in Europe, with massive stockpiles of weapons and ammunitions. The Muslims had no army, no weapons, and no access to any arms shipments, owing to an arms embargo against Yugoslavia. Denied the protection of international forces or the right to raise an army themselves, they were completely defenseless.

Sarajevo remained under siege for four years, cut off from aid by the surrounding mountains.

A tunnel, nearly half a mile (approx. 700–800 m) long, often flooded, and with open electric wire running its length, connected Sarajevo to the UN-controlled area past Butmir Airport. This was Sarajevo's only link to the outside world for over 1,200 days. More than 10,000 people died during the siege, and those who survived had only unreliable and sporadic access to food, water, electricity, and medical supplies.

The UN–EC Peace Plan

Up until 1993, the Croats and the Muslims were united against the Serbs. The Vance-Owen Plan (VOP) attempted to redefine the borders of BiH, Serbia, and Croatia, but ultimately failed when it awarded enormous areas of BiH to Croatia, putting Muslim nationhood at risk. In a secret meeting, Tuđman and Milošević redrew the map, splitting Bosnia between themselves. According to their plan, the Muslim population would be expelled or killed.

The current tensions between Croats and Muslims in Mostar, in Herzegovina, date to a particular set of events in 1993. Although Croatia and Bosnia had formally allied themselves, some Bosnian Croats were angry that Bosnia had resisted becoming part of a larger Croatian–Bosnian state. In an attempt to establish an autonomous region in Herzegovina, with Mostar as its capital, the HVO (the Croat forces) besieged the city for eleven months. All its Muslim inhabitants were to be killed, expelled, or taken under their control. In one instance of effective international involvement, David Hume, then head of UNHCR in Herzegovina, worked tirelessly to bring international attention to the crisis.

As UN peacekeepers were increasingly being targeted by the JNA, the international community started to mobilize. NATO members, frustrated with the UN's lack of involvement, began targeted air strikes against the Serb army in April 1994. After a UN–NATO ultimatum and Russian diplomatic involvement, the leaders of the Serbs, Croats, and

Muslims began negotiations at the Dayton Air Force Base in Ohio in December 1995. An agreement was eventually reached in the form of the Dayton Accords, which granted 49 percent of the territory (RS) to the Serbs and 51 percent to the Croat–Muslim Federation. It was intended to be a temporary solution while Bosnia–Herzegovina wrote a new constitution, but BiH continues to be governed under the arrangements that the Dayton Accords established. Part of this agreement established 60,000 peacekeepers in the region.

Even today, no one really knows what name to give what happened in the 1990s. Although it certainly meets the definition of "genocide," using this term has political implications. It was both a civil war and a sovereignty issue, and the word "conflict" does not really do justice to the tragedies that took place. Most Bosnians simply call it "the war," but be mindful of how you refer to this series of events. At the end of the violence, more than 150,000 people had died, and more than 1.3 million people became refugees.

Despite the atrocities of the war and the strong ethnic lines that were drawn, most Bosnians today wish to live in peace with their neighbors. Many wistfully recall the time when all three groups lived and prospered together. Recovery has been slow, but determined.

The economy has grown, although it remains extremely weak. Shops have reopened and cultural events have resumed. Mobility between the regions is good, but administratively and politically it remains a nightmare. Bosnia is once again at a crossroads, as Croatia moves toward EU membership and Serbia struggles to define its boundaries and alliances. The two entities of Bosnia do little to unite its people, and its constitution must be revised before further progress can take place.

GOVERNMENT AND POLITICS

In response to the communist policies of Tito and the nationalist agendas during the war, BiH has taken democracy to an unwieldy level. It is attempting to become a federal democratic republic, but the bureaucracy of the government is huge, making it difficult to pass even the simplest laws or policies. No one is happy about the system, but to change it would require the cooperation of a vast number of people, few of whom would be willing to risk their positions. Corruption, kickbacks, and nepotism define the political world.

More than fifty political parties are active in BiH, but the main groups are relics of parties that existed during the war: the SDA (mainly Bosniak), the HDZ (Croat), and the SDS (Serbian).

Bosnia is simultaneously ruled by three popularly elected presidents—a Serb, a Croat, and a Bosniak—who share a rotating four-year term. Coordination or cooperation is nearly impossible, as each one is loyal to his voters, who are almost exclusively members of his ethnic group. There is

also a head of government, the Chairman of the Council of Ministers. Several ministries and a cabinet are also involved in state-level government. A bicameral parliament, consisting of a House of Representatives and a House of Peoples, governs at the federal level. The RS and the Federation have regional parliamentary assemblies.

In compliance with the Dayton Accords, the Office of the High Representative (OHR) was established to see that the Accords were being implemented, underwritten by the presence of NATO troops. On paper, the High Representative has absolute power; in practice, he can do very little and is openly defied by Bosnian officials. The original 60,000 troops were succeeded by a smaller NATO stabilization force (SFOR) to deter future hostilities, and in 2004 EU peacekeeping forces (EUFOR) took over with the goal of maintaining peace and stability. These troop levels were reduced from 7,000 to 2,500 in 2007 as their mission shifted from peacekeeping to civil policing. The numbers recently dropped even lower, and the foreign military presence in Bosnia is disappearing.

Many issues are preventing Bosnia from being able to govern itself fully. In addition to bureaucratic struggles, ethnic and nationalist issues make it difficult for politicians to unite. Some in the RS are desirous of either independence or joining Serbia, although this is by no means a universal sentiment. The recent independence of Kosovo, in February 2008, was a tense time for Bosnia, and many feared it would inspire some in the RS to assert their desire for independence. There were a few small rallies in the streets, but the response was much quieter than had been feared. The Brcko District in northwestern Bosnia is still supervised internationally; before the war this region was a mixture of Serbs and Bosniaks, but now it is nearly 99 percent Serb. In addition, police reform remains a major issue, and this is tied to conflicts between the entities. Neither entity wants to give up local powers to the federal level, especially the RS. A police reform act was passed in 2007, which was rewarded by the EU with an SAA (Stabilization and Association Agreement), typically a major step toward EU membership. This happened very quickly, but Bosnia has a long way to go before fulfilling the requirements set out in the SAA. Nothing changed much as a result of either the police reform or the SAA—it was more a pat on the back to Bosnians for trying to address the issue.

The Federation is made up of ten regional cantons whose local government handles taxes, education, public works, and other systematic administration. While the larger, entity-level parliament governs the Federation as a whole, the cantons coordinate trade, health systems, communications, and the military. Within the Federation, each canton has its own court and a number of municipal courts. The RS is governed by its own parliament at an entity level, and relies on municipal governments for local concerns.

There are also two federal-level courts: the BH Constitutional Court and the BH State Court. Obviously, coordinating political or legal matters is very difficult across cantonal or entity borders.

THE BOSNIAN ECONOMY

Under Tito, Bosnia's economy flourished and it seemed poised to become a stable, economically developed country. The war seriously undermined this trend, and the economy still hasn't recovered. There are a number of reasons for this. First, business administration in Bosnia is a bureaucratic nightmare, and it is very difficult to start new businesses, encourage foreign investment, or have various permits approved. Second, unemployment in the country hovers around 40 percent, although gray economy activity probably reduces the levels somewhat. The black market is a thriving part of the Bosnian economy, making it difficult to measure exactly the current status of its economy.

Although more and more young Bosnians are attending universities, there is not a job market to support them, and this has led to a growing class of educated, unemployed, and disillusioned youth. Currently, BiH and Macedonia remain the poorest of the former Yugoslav states, with a GDP per person of around $7,000 a year, and 25 percent of the population below the poverty line.

The economic situation is still uncertain. Nationalist political groups driven by corruption and greed are preventing the necessary reforms from being pushed through. According to the OHR, Bosnia faces a number of specific challenges to its economy, including a complex tax system, barriers to the free movement of goods and people, and a lack of nationwide infrastructural industries, like transport, banking, and energy. The country also lacks both transparency in private business and national economic institutions to regulate them. Complicating issues are the relics of Communism, which have given many Bosnians both a sense of entitlement to certain services, such as jobs and health care, and the feeling that they have no way of obtaining these things themselves.

Bosnian farms are small, but provide a good source of fresh vegetables, fruit, and meat. The rest of its food staples are imported. Bosnian currency is called the convertible mark (BAM, or KM), and is tied to the euro at a 2:1 ratio. Foreign banks mainly control the banking industry, and confidence in the currency is growing.

As time passes, BiH will receive less and less international aid, and will probably experience a difficult adjustment period as it is reduced. High unemployment, a haphazard privatization process,

and a large account deficit also make the economic picture rather bleak. There is economic potential in the country, however, especially in terms of ecotourism, exports of mineral water, and a sizeable industrial economy that includes coal, steel, iron ore, salt, and hydropower.

BOSNIA IN EUROPE

In general, Bosnia is pro-Europe and tries to be very Western-minded. As EU member countries push east, with the recent admissions of Romania and Bulgaria, and Croatian membership anticipated in 2010, Bosnia is trying hard to align itself with pro-Europe policies. It has a long way to go, however, and some fundamental changes in its constitution must take place before this can happen.

At present Bosnians are somewhat cut off from their European neighbors because of travel restrictions. They must apply for visas to travel abroad, which is a lengthy and time-consuming process. On a large scale, this seriously hinders economic and intellectual cooperation.

Bosnia remains an untapped resource in terms of tourism and economic potential, and this will surely gain prominence as the millennium progresses. It remains a strategic area as the Balkans continues to attempt to define itself. The recent independence of Kosovo and the struggle of ideologies in Serbia indicate that this region is not yet politically settled.

BOSNIANS AROUND THE WORLD

Between the Second World War and the war of the 1990s, many Bosnians fled the country. Today, there is a general attrition of educated, professional people who can find better jobs and living conditions elsewhere. Although this has implications for Bosnia's future, it also means that there are more than a million Bosnians all over the world who can draw attention to this small country with big potential. The United States is home to many Bosnians, primarily in New York, Boston, and, the largest community, St. Louis. There are communities in Canada, the UK, Austria, Australia, Sweden, Germany, Italy, Turkey, and many other countries.

chapter two

VALUES &
ATTITUDES

There are differences between Croats, Serbs, and
Bosniaks, and the war redistributed the population
so that towns are more ethnically homogeneous.
However, the overarching Bosnian values—
friendliness, family, and hospitality—are universal.

For all the talk about ethnic differences in
Bosnia, a glance around the street will reveal a
crowd of rather similar-looking people. Bosnians
tend to be slender, with dark hair and eyes, like
many of their Mediterranean cousins. Bosnian
fashion is quite dressy, and men and women alike
wear trendy clothes. Although many people live
on meager incomes, a lot of money is spent on
personal appearance, and nice clothes are a major
status symbol.

Bosnians are friendly, open, and extremely
hospitable. They enjoy a good laugh, a cup of
strong coffee, and the company of family and
friends. The average Bosnian cares deeply for the
welfare of his close circle friends and family.
Bosnians tend to have a rather pessimistic view of
their circumstances and their country's future, but
are proud of local specialties, like their strong
liquor, the beautiful landscape, and the historical

significance of the country. The average Bosnian probably smokes, takes regular coffee breaks, and has strong opinions about the political or economic situation. There is a clear generation gap, with Bosnian youth embracing Western culture wholeheartedly while the older population is more conservative.

In sum, Bosnians are friendly and generous, and their warmth makes it easy to feel at home.

RELIGIOUS VALUES

Despite a history of secularism under Tito, religious values are still extremely important in Bosnia and are a defining characteristic of the people. While for some people religion is little more than a marker of one's heritage, others are quite devout. Most Bosnians lie somewhere in the middle, with religious values driving family values and cultural norms, but not necessarily forming an all-encompassing part of daily life. Note that while religious affiliation typically defines one's ethnic affiliation, this is not exclusively true. For example, around 48 percent of the population are Bosniaks, but only around 40 percent of the population practice Islam.

Despite the huge numbers of Bosnian Muslims killed in the wars of the twentieth century, Muslim culture is still very vibrant in Bosnia. Muslim education and religious societies are extremely active, and produce some of the best schools and cultural events in the country. Traditional Bosnian Islam is somewhat secular, and it is only recently that more traditional forms of Islam have gained a foothold in Bosnia. One little-discussed fact is where the money for such programs comes from. The Bosnian form of Islam is quite Western and very tolerant, and a beautiful example of how Muslim culture can coexist with Western values. However, there is some concern from the international community about money coming into Islamic organizations from the Middle East, especially from Wahhabi sources. Wahhabism is a strict and controversial form of Islam that originated in Saudi Arabia and has been gaining worldwide influence through the sponsoring of Islamic programs abroad. It is not yet known how alliances with this branch of Islam will affect Bosnian Islam, but some of the money that comes into these programs comes with conditions for how the programs will be run. As a result, the conservative influence of Wahhabism is visible in some places. All indications, however, show that most Bosniaks remain extremely open, tolerant, and faithful, and it is to be hoped that this trend will continue.

Catholicism is still a major part of many Bosnians' lives, especially in Croatian-bordered

Herzegovina. Today, only about 15 percent of the population is Catholic, but their contributions to Bosnian culture are far-reaching. Međjugorje, just outside Mostar, hosts one of the most-visited Catholic

pilgrimage sites in Europe, and it holds a special place in the hearts of many Bosnian Catholics. Catholics in Bosnia are proud of their religious affiliation and show this through their observance; along with the daily calls to prayer in the mosques, the Sunday bells peal in downtown Sarajevo and the streets fill with churchgoers in their Sunday best.

Orthodox Christianity is mainly prevalent in the

RS, and Orthodox Bosnians make up 31 percent of the population (the Serb population is slightly higher, around 37 percent). Orthodox cathedrals are some of the most beautiful religious edifices in the country, and Orthodox Christianity has a long, rich history here.

On the whole, all of the three religious groups are very aware of their neighbors and extremely tolerant of their right to practice. Croats and Serbs know all about Ramadan and Bajram, and share in the festive atmosphere during these times. Muslims are perfectly tolerant of Christmas decorations in December, and respect the faithfulness of their neighbors. There are exceptions, of course, mostly in the older generation or in some rural pockets of BiH, but any expression of intolerance is generally taboo. In addition, religious values are somewhat fluid. For example, young girls who wear the veil and attend *medresas*—Islamic schools—might take off their veils when they hang out with their friends. People are eager to live in peace once again, and some of the best examples of rebuilding of trust between ethnic groups have happened on an individual level.

Unfortunately, there is still some intolerance—mostly lack of understanding—for faiths outside the three major groups. Anyone who looks "different" will be singled out; ethnic slurs are a frequent part of Bosnian humor, but are occasionally used with the intent to insult. The Jewish population in Bosnia is extremely small, and is getting smaller every year. To call someone a "Jew" is an enormous insult, even today. In addition, many Bosnians are influenced by international news media, especially about the Middle East.

Most Bosnian Muslims are sympathetic to the Palestinian cause. There is a consensus in Bosnia that Israel, and therefore Jewish people, are responsible for violence in the Middle East, and therefore violence against Muslims. This is by no means universal, and especially not in Sarajevo.

Ingrained Attitudes

After visiting a mosque with some *medresa* students, one of the girls calmly explained to me that she didn't like Jews, and that although she had enjoyed attending a Jewish dinner I had hosted, her parents had instructed her not to eat the food. I asked her how many Jews she knew, and she replied, "Just you, but I like you, so it's confusing." Where this opinion persists, it generally isn't out of a desire to annihilate the Jews, but rather a misguided belief that that's simply how things are. Most expressions of intolerance toward Jews and other groups are primarily based on ignorance and may not even intend to offend.

Naturally, there are many well-educated and tolerant people of all faiths in Bosnia. As BiH continues to move toward the West, and as new peoples and ideas come to the country, it is to be hoped that tolerance will continue to grow.

THE LEGACY OF COMMUNISM

The legacy of communism is most strongly evident in the workplace. Many Bosnians

remember the time when everyone had a job, an education, and access to health care, and are frustrated with the high unemployment and lack of efficient social services today. Communism is remembered as a time of job security, and some members of the older generation are struggling to adjust to an economy that becomes more capitalist every day. The younger generation is starting to change this trend, but progress is slow. It is hard to blame Bosnians for their nostalgia; under Tito, jobs were easy to find and maintain, overtime was unheard of, and social services were burgeoning. The sudden shift in the way business is conducted means that some Bosnians are apathetic or unmotivated, and many are lost without direct instructions from their bosses.

Mind-numbing bureaucracy and an overstaffed government are other relics of the past. Power hierarchies continue to be important, and little has changed in the public sector in terms of how business is done—and sometimes not even the furniture.

Attitudes toward education and learning also bear the influences of Communism. Especially in the universities, education is fact based, rather than analytical. Students are rarely encouraged to think for themselves, memorizing vast amounts of information, but with little opportunity to apply it critically during their studies.

THE LEGACY OF THE WAR

The tragedy and lasting impact of the war in Bosnia–Herzegovina cannot be overstated. It redefined the population, the government, the borders, and the economy. However, it ended more than thirteen years ago, and is still frequently touted as an excuse for the current predicament. While it certainly led to many of the problems that exist today, the continuing problems are more a result of a feeling of lack of control over one's environment and a resulting apathy. Change is possible, but Bosnians are not showing the kind of self-initiative that true progress requires, and government officials are often more concerned with being reelected than in cooperating with their opponents. Many continue to excuse the current situation by looking back, keeping Bosnia from looking forward. Sadly, there are few signs of this changing any time soon.

When a colleague or friend starts telling stories about the war, it can often shut down the discussion. Every adult in Bosnia has experienced truly awful circumstances as a result of the war, but some also use the war as a "get out of jail free" card or an attempt to excuse away their difficulties today, whether it's appropriate or not. After thirteen years, many Bosnians still feel disempowered, and it shows every day.

WORK ETHIC

The Bosnian view of hard work is slightly different from American or European conceptions of the words. Many Bosnians work extremely hard to support their families, but this does not always extend to the workplace. This attitude is probably a combination of hangovers from the Communist era, as well as a general apathy that results from the lack of jobs. More so, many of the jobs that are available tend neither to pay well nor to offer opportunities for advancement, so there is less incentive to work overtime. Clearly, this varies with private sector jobs and jobs at international organizations.

Bosnians highly value personal time, an indication of the role the family plays in society. Those who have jobs do not work fourteen-hour days—nor would they want to. Like their Italian neighbors, they espouse a balance of work and play. Their general well-being relies on having time for coffee with friends or for vacations with family. Also, there are in Bosnia many disabled or ill people, either as a result of the war or because of the poor quality of health care. Many people spend at least some of their time caring for older relatives or helping out with children. Thus, although Bosnians may not be career driven as a whole, they are certainly busy with many obligations, so it would be unfair to assume they have a poor work ethic—which some foreigners, judging by how crowded the cafés are in the daytime, might be tempted to do.

ATTITUDES TOWARD FOREIGNERS

The failure of the UN peacekeepers to protect
people during the war and the longtime presence
of NATO troops mean that Bosnians, especially in
Sarajevo, have strong opinions about foreigners.
Many are justifiably angry that the international
community did so little to intervene at the start of
the conflict. After the economy started to recover,
however, many became conditioned to, and in
some ways, reliant on the international presence
for the management of the country.

The Dayton Accords were intended to be
provisional, yet they still determine how the
country is run. Diplomatic missions, the UNHCR,
USAID, the World Bank, and the OSCE are still
major presences. Bosnians work for these
organizations, but rarely in management positions,
which means that, in many ways, foreigners run
the country. Nonetheless, jobs in the international
sector are sought after for their higher wages and
better working conditions. English is becoming
increasingly widely spoken, and despite the
sometimes complicated dynamics of power
distribution, there is a healthy friendship between
internationals and their Bosnian coworkers.

Despite their pessimism about the state of
their country, Bosnians are proud. Foreigners who
put on airs, or act in a superior way, will quickly
make enemies. The Americans and the British are
especially known for this. Visitors should be very
careful to show respect for Bosnian culture and
not give Bosnians the impression that they

believe they are superior, or know better. Don't treat Bosnia as a developing country or as a backwater—it is neither.

On an individual basis, Bosnians welcome foreigners, especially if they approach Bosnian culture with respect and sympathy. Anyone who looks different from the Balkan physiognomy will draw curious glances and remarks, although these are probably not meant in an offensive way. Blacks and Asians are not commonly seen in the area. As Bosnians are not shy, they will probably ask you where you are from, or make an interested comment on your difference of appearance.

A Wise Ambassador

Several times a day, a good—and very patient—Asian American friend of mine would have mock Chinese shouted at her whenever she walked down the street. She would always just smile or engage in conversation with the individual concerned, becoming a wonderful ambassador for her country in the process.

As one might expect, there are numbers of Croats and Serbs in Bosnia, but there are also minority groups from other countries. There are many Germans—German is widely spoken among the older generations—and Italians, and there is a Chinese community outside Sarajevo, with shops selling Chinese products.

FAMILY MATTERS

The family is by far the most important social unit in Bosnia. The family counts above all else, and Bosnians have close and frequent contact with their extended family, all of whom tend to live near enough to visit each other frequently. Children are highly valued and indulged, and are the center of attention at family gatherings.

Although many Bosnian men and women support gender equality, the practice is a little bit different. Men are still the head of the household and make most of the major decisions. Most Bosnian men prefer "real women"—those who are nurturing and domestic. "Real men" don't do the housework or cooking.

The dichotomy is difficult to explain. Women make up the majority of students at the universities, many have careers, and are encouraged in this, but even "liberated" women tend to marry relatively young, have children, and take care of the home. Femininity in the traditional sense is highly valued, and many women take pride in their ability to take care of their families. On the other hand, while "macho" men are not necessarily seen as the ideal, this attitude is still indulged. Women still make much less money than men, and traditional gender roles extend to the workplace. These gender roles are not necessarily rigid, because men and women who don't conform to them are not ostracized, but most men and women in Bosnia

culture smart! bosnia and herzegovina

seem to be happy fulfilling the traditional gender roles, while there are accepted avenues for career-minded women and for domestic-minded men.

MINORITY GROUPS

There are two groups within Bosnia that require special mention: the local mafia organizations, and the Roma population. Organized crime is a huge problem, and permeates all sections of society, including the government. The cost of this is estimated at between 150 and 300 million euros—the same amount as the state's annual budget. The crimes committed range from violent gang behavior to sophisticated embezzlement and fraud, involving a huge siphoning off of tax revenue and foreign aid. The Bosnian police forces are not sufficiently equipped to handle this, and international forces have made few inroads on the issue. While there are some international mafia organizations, including Russian and Albanian groups, the strongest are locally based. These groups are brazen, especially in the context of the living standards of average Bosnians. Be wary of people driving flashy cars or wearing expensive suits—they may not be the best ones to make deals with.

At the other end of the economic spectrum are the Roma, the gypsy population. Roma numbers are difficult to project, as they rarely participate in government censuses, but upper estimates put them at around 50,000. The Roma have suffered horribly throughout history, and have never had a state to call home or find refuge in. Communism abolished their nomadic culture, capitalism eliminated their traditional economy (including handicrafts and horse dealing), and widespread xenophobia prevents even those who wish to assimilate from doing so. The Roma today remain justifiably wary of the mainstream, but this has served only to hamstring them further as their children go uneducated and most of the group live in abject poverty.

You will see Roma children all over Bosnia, and sympathy for their plight can fade rather quickly in the wake of their very persistent requests for "*jedna marka*" (one mark). It is up to you whether you wish to give money or not; most Bosnians do so just to get them to go away, but it is probably better to buy them a sandwich, or the money will end up in the hands of the head of the family. It is a dreadful situation, and children as young as three or four can often be seen begging for money in the middle of a busy intersection. Mothers will thrust their babies into the arms of a passer-by while attempting to steal a purse or wallet. Roma teenagers are under wide suspicion, for they routinely attempt to rob when an opportunity arises. It is a culture that is wholly at odds with the rest of Bosnian society, making it difficult to generate public sympathy, although they desperately need help and education.

BRIBERY AND CORRUPTION

Corruption and bribery dominate all aspects of
Bosnian business and politics. It is still possible to
get things done by giving the right person money
or, more commonly, through having the right

connections. To some degree
this is accepted, with people
relying on family members to
get them jobs. Personal
recommendations count for
everything. Foreigners may

find it difficult to get permits or open bank
accounts unless they have a Bosnian friend to open
the door for them. On a macro scale, the political
system is rife with corruption that severely hinders
transparency and EU aspirations.

There are going rates for certain services but it
is difficult for an outsider to know when and
where this applies. On a small, everyday scale,
bribes are commonly used to get out of paying
speeding fines, or to get paperwork processed. On
the other hand, there are many, many honest
Bosnians with unfailing integrity, so don't
assume the worst too quickly. This sort of
behavior is becoming increasingly unacceptable,
especially by educated Bosnians and young,
Western-minded individuals.

THE GENERATION GAP

There is a large divide between the young and the
older generations in BiH. Although young people

remain family oriented and maintain the best of Bosnian values—hospitality and friendliness—they tend to be more focused on their education, more career minded, and more Western oriented than their parents. The transition is by no means complete, however, so one cannot easily predict where any particular young person might stand on a specific issue. Religious values continue to be important, although young people tend to be more tolerant and open-minded than their parents.

On the whole, it is best not to make assumptions. Some young people are open to religious tolerance but don't believe in evolution or tolerate homosexuality. Some older adults might be very career oriented, but still maintain traditional ideas on gender roles.

THE URBAN–RURAL GAP

One of the biggest insults one can give is to say someone is "village," or "from the villages." This means that the individual is provincial, narrow-minded, or stupid. It is a stereotype built on the fact that rural communities tend to be more ethnically homogeneous, be less mobile, and have less easy access to new ideas. The economic conditions of the rural populations are lower, and life can be very difficult for them. City folk, especially those in Sarajevo, can be a bit snobbish in their sense of superiority over rural people, although most of them probably have family somewhere in rural Bosnia.

SUPERSTITIONS

Bosnians are a superstitious people and tend to believe in fate. Although all cultures have their superstitions, Americans and Western Europeans tend to view their own with some skepticism. Bosnians, on the other hand, see certain things as fact. Even though certain traditional beliefs might seem silly to foreigners, it would be insulting to call them "superstitions." There is a certain sense of powerlessness in Bosnian culture, and the Arabic phrase "*inshallah*" (God willing) encapsulates this idea, as in, "I won't run out of gas before getting to work, *inshallah*." The lines between superstition and belief are blurred, and in some cases, folk wisdom has become truth. Natural remedies are an excellent example of this. Some are probably effective, at least psychologically, while others seem downright fanciful. Don't be surprised if the doctor at the biggest hospital in the country prescribes rubbing a brandy-soaked cloth over your chest when you have a sore throat. To get rid of a fever, some mothers may wrap their children's feet in vodka-soaked rags with a potato.

One good example of this sort of folk wisdom is the dreaded effects of a cold draft, or "*propuh*." Bosnians strongly believe that being exposed to a draft, or getting one's feet wet, will result in illness. They believe, in a very literal sense, that "cold" is there to be caught—that one will "catch cold." They are convinced that you *will* get sick if you leave the house with wet hair, and that women should be especially careful to avoid getting chilled because their ovaries might freeze, causing infertility (seriously). Bosnians tend not to leave windows open or wear open-toed shoes unless it is very warm. Children are bundled up with clothes even in warm weather. As a foreigner, you will draw attention if you don't dress warmly enough by their standards.

The evil eye is still a prevalent superstition, and if a person receives the evil eye, he may suffer sickness, property damage, or even death. The evil eye is Turkish in origin, and mainly a Muslim superstition. A great number of ills and discomforts may be attributed to the evil eye, and you may frequently see a blue stone with an eye painted in the middle to deflect ill intentions. These make popular refrigerator magnets.

Fortune-telling is popular in Bosnia, mainly among older women. Fortune-tellers read the grounds from Turkish coffee, a person's hand, or an arrangement of beans of any kind. This sort of behavior is more common among friends drinking coffee at home than in a crowded, downtown café.

chapter three

HOLIDAYS & CELEBRATIONS

Considering the range of religious and ethnic groups in the country, it comes as no surprise that a variety of holidays are celebrated, but few bring the country together as a whole. However, all groups are aware of the major holidays and traditions of the others and, on the whole, respect their observance. The celebration of holidays varies widely among ethnic groups, among regions of the country, and in the case of religious holidays between individuals also, according to their piety.

In general, holidays are a time for family and friends. Most Bosnians are happy to share their special times with foreigners, and will be all too glad to help them understand their traditions.

RAMADAN

Ramadan is a forty-day Muslim holiday in which people fast from dawn until nightfall. It is a time of penitence and prayer, when Muslims ask God for forgiveness and guidance. Ramadan falls in the ninth month of the Islamic year, which operates on a lunar calendar; therefore the dates change from year to year. The fast is strictly kept, and observers do not even sip water during the day. Despite this, observant Muslims still go to work and to school. In areas of the country where Ramadan is widely practiced, some schools will schedule their opening dates after Ramadan ends.

BAJRAM

Bajram is a major Muslim holiday that comes twice a year. Eid ul-Fitr occurs at the end of Ramadan, and is a celebration of the end of the fast season. Literally translated as "festival for the breaking of the fast," it is marked by feasting and general revelry. It is celebrated over several days with family and friends. Best clothes are worn, and gifts are given to the poor.

The second Bajram, Eid al-Adha, occurs about seventy days later, during the time when some Muslims are on pilgrimage to Mecca. Eid al-Adha means "festival of the sacrifice," and is a celebration of God's mercy when Abraham vowed to sacrifice his son.

For both holidays, many schools and businesses close. In contrast, Bosnian businesses may only close for a day or two at Christmas, but Bajram usually results in several days off. Muslims often travel around the country to visit their families during these times. According to Bosnian law, everyone may take up to four days off for religious holidays, but not all religious holidays are an inherent part of the business calendar.

Foreigners may be invited to celebrate Bajram with new friends on either occasion, and this should be considered a big honor, similar to inviting a friend to an American Thanksgiving with your family or to Christmas dinner. Don't expect to get a lot of business deals completed during either Bajram celebration, but be sure to enjoy the festive atmosphere.

CHRISTMAS

Christmas in Bosnia is generally a much quieter affair than in the rest of Europe, and much less than in America. While Christmas trees and other decorations may be visible in some shops, it does not induce the same sort of shopping frenzy as it does elsewhere. *Djed mraz* (literally, "Grandpa Frost") visits children and brings gifts, regardless of religion, although some traditional Muslims may not follow this practice.

There are in fact two Christmases in Bosnia, depending on whether one is Catholic or Orthodox. The Catholic Christmas falls on December 25, and the Orthodox one on January 7. Catholic holidays follow the Gregorian calendar, introduced by Pope Gregory XVIII in 1582, while Orthodox Christians observe the Julian calendar, instituted by Julius Caesar in 46 BCE. Bosnian employees may take time off for either holiday, but businesses generally remain open during this time.

NEW YEAR

As with Christmas, Catholics and Orthodox Christians celebrate the New Year on different days: Catholics on January 1 and Orthodox Christians on January 14. Generally, January 1 is more widely celebrated, but in the RS there are more instances of the later date being observed.

The New Year is characterized by a general feeling of celebration. Friends get together for big parties, with food and dancing. People like to set off fireworks, and some of the bigger cities put on displays. As the tradition goes, how you spend New Year's Eve determines the rest of the year to come. Girls kiss their boyfriends at midnight to make sure they stay together for the coming year; people wear gold to ensure a prosperous year; or dress up in red in the hope of romance.

MAY HOLIDAY

Officially known as Labor Day, this is generally referred to as the May holiday. It usually coincides with the first instance of good weather, so many people take this time to go on vacation to the coast.

INDEPENDENCE DAY

Independence Day falls on March 1 and celebrates Bosnian independence from Yugoslavia in 1992. This is a national holiday, and businesses are closed. Observance of the day is generally quiet, but you may see cars driving down the road with flags streaming from the windows and horns blaring. Some Serbian Bosnians do not celebrate the day, particularly those in the RS. They feel that Bosnia should be part of a Greater Yugoslavia, or that the RS should be its own state; however, this sentiment varies from place to place.

January 9, an important saint's day in the Christian Orthodox calendar, has been designated Republika Srpska Day. This is a politically charged holiday, ignored in the Federation and celebrated to varying degrees by Serbs in the RS. Most Bosnians think it's a pity that Independence Day isn't celebrated by all Bosnians, and that state unity should be the ultimate goal. Until the entity issue is resolved, however, this holiday is likely to carry political weight.

EASTER

Easter is an important holiday for Christians, and for the pious, a time of religious fervor. The faithful attend mass. Many people take the opportunity to make a pilgrimage to the shrine of the Blessed Virgin Mary in Međjugorje, in Herzegovina.

More secular Bosnians see Easter as a time to get together with their families and enjoy a good meal. It is traditional to exchange decorated eggs, and a popular game is for two people to crack eggs together to see whose breaks first.

BIRTHDAYS

The celebration of birthdays in BiH does not differ much from the rest of Europe and North America. They are an opportunity for individuals to spend time with friends and family and be singled out for a day. Cakes, parties, and presents are all common. However, it is typical for the birthday boy or girl to treat his or her guests to drinks or dinner, rather than the other way around.

WEDDINGS

Weddings are a big deal in Bosnia. Since family is the root of the social structure, and divorce is not common, weddings are celebrated with especial pomp in this region.

A wedding is an excuse to bring families together and to demonstrate the hospitality of the hosts. It is not unusual to invite two hundred guests, and sometimes there are many more.

After the ceremony, the wedding party drives through the town in cars decked with ribbons and flowers. The drivers wave flags and honk mercilessly to announce the happy event. At the reception there will be plentiful food and often a band. Rural marriages are usually much bigger affairs than urban weddings, and can last for several days; but of course the scale depends on the wealth of the family. It is usual to bring a

gift for the new couple, although gift registries are not common. A long-standing Muslim tradition was to present the couple with a handwoven rug (*kilim*) with their initials and wedding date woven into it. Sadly, these beautiful examples of local handicraft are rapidly disappearing.

Serbs tend to put on luxurious weddings in order to usher in happiness and wealth for the new couple. Rather than rice, they throw wheat grains to ensure fertility.

Happily, most, if not all, marriages in Bosnia today are love matches, and nearly a third of urban marriages are interethnic. The average age of marriage is about twenty-three, but working professionals, especially women, often postpone marriage until their early thirties.

BIRTH

On the birth of a child the celebrations vary according to religion, but in a family-centered culture this is naturally an occasion for great joy, and there are parties, feasts, and gift giving—though baby showers are uncommon, and festivities are generally reserved until after the birth. Then friends and family visit with gifts of clothes or food.

In Bosnian Muslim tradition, boys are circumcised at the age of three. This event is preceded by a feast and a number of festivities.

In the Christian Orthodox and Catholic traditions a baby is baptized, with the godparent naming the child at the ceremony. Godparents take their role seriously, and are considered to be part of the family. After the baptismal ceremony there is a big celebration, with food and dancing.

Abortion is legal in Bosnia during the first ten weeks of pregnancy, but is taboo for religious reasons. Sex outside marriage is frowned upon (the practice is somewhat different, however), and a child born out of wedlock is stigmatized. If a woman becomes pregnant, the couple is expected to marry.

DEATH

Beliefs about death vary by religion, but most people are buried rather than cremated. Cemeteries are consequently large. Muslim tombstones have a distinctive shape—thin and narrow, and curved on top. Sarajevo is full of cemeteries with tombstone after tombstone dating from the 1992–95 period.

Muslims and Christians alike wear black in mourning, and rely heavily on their families for support. In Muslim tradition, families gather at home to mourn. There are forty days of mourning, during which time women cover their heads; they do not attend the funeral, but stay at home to *tevhid,* or pray for the dead. During this period families may avoid watching TV at  home, and friends often bring them coffee or food.

chapter four

MAKING FRIENDS

When you have made friends with a Bosnian, you have formed a relationship that will last a lifetime. Loyalty to friends is of the utmost importance, and friendships are nurtured with great care. You may be surprised at the obligations involved, however, and it is important to be aware of expectations, so as not to offend.

A close friend is treated as part of the family.

The friendship requires more than just a monthly phone call or yearly visit, and your friend will be hurt if you turn down too many invitations, or accept and don't reciprocate. Friends keep in close contact and spend a great deal of time with each other, often simply dropping by or meeting after exchanging a text or two.

Generally, friendships in Bosnia are locally based and centered on family and religious groups, often broadened to include classmates and neighbors. Bosnians don't travel around much, and prefer to stay near their loved ones. This means that circles of friends often belong to the same religious or ethnic group, although this is not always the case in cities.

Foreigners are generally welcomed with open arms into Bosnian circles, and will be made to feel at home at once. Bosnians are genuinely interested in their friends from abroad, and there are rarely hidden agendas to the warmth they show them. The best way to become a part of a group is to return their hospitality in full force. Invite them to your home, take them out to lunch or coffee, and keep in regular contact with them. To do less would be an insult. While friendships tend to require more involvement than most Westerners are used to, the rewards are enormous; these people will befriend you forever, and will offer support and encouragement with gusto. In keeping with this spirit, the personal recommendation of a friend means quite a lot, and is an instant "in" in business circles; indeed, it is really one of the only ways to do effective business in the country.

SOCIABILITY
On the whole, Bosnians are fond of conversation and lingering over coffee. They will be curious about your life back home, and may be amazed that you have chosen to travel so far from your family and friends. They will share stories about

their own families in turn, as well as talking about their work or other concerns. Sports are a favorite topic among men, and music and movies are popular all around. Young Bosnians like to talk about movies, music, boyfriends and girlfriends, and all the usual topics of conversation you might expect. Many young people are interested in astrology, and will ask your star sign when you are first getting acquainted.

Bosnians are enthusiastic matchmakers, and will inquire bluntly about whether or not you are married. If you befriend a Bosnian family and reveal that you are single, don't be surprised if unattached cousins and grandchildren suddenly appear for dinner! It won't matter if they can speak English or not.

There is a concern that foreign men may corrupt their daughters and abandon them, so if you are a single man you may be viewed with some suspicion. Dating is a serious business in Bosnia, and most people marry young. If a long-term attachment does develop, however, the parents are likely to be overjoyed at the prospect of their child having a stable, salaried husband.

Dating progresses slowly here. A potential couple will eye each other for a month, then they might go out for coffee with a group of friends before finally agreeing to meet one-to-one. If you as a woman are forthcoming with men, you might be perceived as "easy"—the men will certainly respond positively, but will perhaps have undesired expectations.

MEETING BOSNIANS

It can be difficult to find a social circle in Bosnia, as people tend to go out in groups and not strike up conversations with strangers in bars or cafés. If you go to a café alone, you will be left to enjoy your coffee in peace. If you go to a bar or club alone, however, you will certainly stand out and will probably spend the evening alone, getting odd stares from those around you. This doesn't mean that Bosnians are unfriendly; on the contrary, they will respond warmly if you introduce yourself. Just don't expect to be approached.

The best way to meet people is to accept invitations from colleagues. Seek out others who are in your situation and who have been there longer than you have; they will understand the difficulties in meeting people and may be able to help you. If you are staying in a hostel, talk to the other travelers and pool your resources. Local diplomatic missions also tend to be close-knit, both in the workplace and socially, and someone in this community will be able to introduce you to a number of locals and internationals alike. Listen for a familiar language in a café, and don't be afraid to introduce yourself—we've all been through it.

BOSNIAN NAMES

In Bosnia, a person's name often indicates their ethnic background. Certain first names and surnames are associated with Bosniaks, Serbians, or Croatians. For example, common Bosniak surnames include Hodžic, Suljević, and Mustafić; typical Serb names might be Mitrović, Vlajković, or Ignjatović; common Croat names are Marić, Brkić, or Pehić. In the city, where there is a great range of people and widespread tolerance, this serves little more purpose than to indicate a fact about a person. In the countryside, where most towns are more homogeneous, the "wrong" name can be justification for a cold shoulder, or worse. While on the whole most people are tolerant, there are exceptions. Additionally, social groups tend to consist of a single ethnic group. Don't be entirely surprised if a Bosnian raises an eyebrow when you mention a certain friend's name.

BOSNIAN HOSPITALITY

Bosnian hospitality is famous. Travelers may be surprised at the generosity of their new friends and hosts, especially considering the difficult economic situation of the country. After meeting you, Bosnians will want to take you out for coffee or will invite you to their home. They will very likely offer you some sort of gift to welcome you. These can include traditional crafts or homemade liquor or preserves.

If a new acquaintance asks you out for coffee, it means they would like to be friends and they will probably offer to pay. It is polite to let them.

If you wish to continue the relationship, be sure to follow up soon with an invitation of your own; this time, you will be expected to pay. It is not common for casual acquaintances to go out for a meal together, so if you are invited to one, it is a particular show of affection, respect, or intention. This is often a way of thanking someone or of sealing a business deal. Whoever does the inviting is expected to pay for the meal.

VISITING A BOSNIAN HOME

You will probably be invited to visit the homes of your new Bosnian friends. This is a special gesture of intimacy, and you should be prepared for the royal treatment—Bosnians lay out a kingly spread for visitors, and go to great lengths to make their guests feel comfortable.

Bring a gift with you—but note some rules. Flowers are a good idea, but make sure you bring an odd number; even numbers are for funerals. Don't bring roses, as these have a romantic connotation. Chocolates or candies are also appreciated, especially if there are children in the house. Wine is a common gift, but make sure your host isn't Muslim before you bring alcohol, and that also goes for pork products, and anything related to dogs. Foreigners can bring a small token from their home: popular gifts are scarves, postcards with pictures of home, or small souvenirs. Knives or other sharp objects should not be given, as they symbolize a severing of the relationship. Gifts should be wrapped. If you are offered a gift, be sure to reciprocate as soon as possible.

It is customary to remove your shoes when entering a Bosnian home. You may be offered a pair of slippers to wear, and it is polite to accept them. Even for a casual visit, you will probably be offered coffee and cigarettes right away. If you stay for a meal, expect a feast. They are likely to start by serving *rakia* (a strong local brandy), coffee, or soda, and a variety of nuts or other small snacks, probably followed by soup, a main dish, and dessert. Afterward, there will be more coffee and probably more *rakia*. Propose a toast and thank them for their hospitality using the phrase "*Zivjeliv!*" ("Cheers!"). The best compliment you can give is to eat as much as possible; leaving food on the plate is an insult. Meals can last several hours, so don't make plans for later. If you are a vegetarian, mention this in advance, and your hosts will be happy to provide something suitable. They will genuinely want to please you, and will be upset if they can't fill you up with whatever they've prepared.

When you leave, your host may give you a gift of wine, homemade food, or some small trinket. The best way of thanking them is to show enthusiastic gratitude and a reciprocal invitation to visit your home. You can also invite them out to dinner, and of course you will be expected to foot the bill.

THE ALL-IMPORTANT COFFEE

Coffee is a ubiquitous part of the country's culture. It is a part of every Bosnian day—often several parts. It is a sign of hospitality and of friendship. When you meet a new friend, you will inevitably be asked out for coffee; if you are making a new business connection, you will be served coffee at meetings or asked to go to one of their favorite cafés. Many Bosnians will have

four or more cups of the stuff a day, slowly savored with friends. Coffee is a hugely important part of Bosnian culture, and you simply will not fit in if you

don't partake in this way of life.

The traditional drink is *bosanska kafa,* a thick, bitter drink served black or with milk, with coffee grounds in the bottom. It's similar to Turkish coffee. Don't feel obliged to order this if you find it too strong for your tastes: espresso, cappuccino, Nescafé (often known just as "Nes"), tea, and fruit juice are all available in most cafés. Coffee is served in much smaller portions than in America, so order a *velika* (large) if you want a portion resembling what you're used to at home. If you are offered coffee in someone's house or office, always accept it—it is impolite to refuse.

How to Drink Bosnian Coffee

Understanding the proper steps to drinking traditional Bosnian coffee will make the experience a lot simpler (and tastier).

The coffee will be served on a metal tray, with a coffeepot, a small cup, and a glass of water. If you order it *sa mlijekom* (with milk), there will be a small cup of milk on the tray as well. There will generally be several lumps of sugar on the tray, and perhaps a piece of *rahatlokum,* similar to Turkish delight.

To begin, pick up the spoon and stir the top of the coffee in the coffeepot until it changes to a light brown color. Only then should you pour it slowly into your cup. You have several options at this point. You can drop in a lump or two of sugar, add milk, or simply drink it straight. Bosnians generally put the sugar cube on a spoon, dip it into the coffee, and eat it. If the cup is resting in a copper holder, leave this on the table—simply lift the porcelain cup out of the holder.

Drink slowly. It's strong stuff, and you're supposed to linger over your cup. When you finish, there is generally enough in the pot to pour another half cup or so. Be careful when pouring a second cup, as the bottom of the coffeepot will be full of coffee grounds. Enjoy!

Love and the Foreigner

After a wild night out, one of your new friends might invite you for coffee the next day. In Bosnian culture, this is often code for a date. Bosnians take dating seriously, and may find foreigners to be both intriguing and somewhat dangerous (at least in the sense of the potential for heartbreak). Be sensitive to this cultural feature to avoid hurt feelings; when in doubt, opt for group settings. Otherwise, you might end up as I did—having coffee with a Bosnian man I'd just met, who's asking me to come over and cook dinner for him that night, and suggesting that maybe the time has finally come to meet his mother!

chapter five

THE BOSNIANS AT HOME

Daily life in Bosnia flows along at a relaxed pace, punctuated with many coffee breaks and leisure time with friends and family. It is certainly a pleasant way of life, and Bosnians generally make the most of it, within their economic constraints. As a foreigner, you may find yourself panicking to realize that you're actually happy working no more than a forty-hour week. It's easy to enjoy the slower pace of life in this part of the world, and to start to wonder if, as fast-paced Westerners, we're missing something despite our jam-packed schedules.

THE BOSNIAN FAMILY

Bosnian families tend to be close-knit and patriarchal. Traditional gender roles are still very much in play. Families often live near each other, although some members may have emigrated outside the country during the war. Holidays are opportunities for families to reunite and reconnect. Women are expected to marry and have children, generally in their twenties, although some are continuing their education and marrying later. Men are typically the head of the household and hold authority, although many women will work if they can find a job. Sadly, as a result of the war and deficiencies in the health care system, it is not uncommon for some families to be missing one or both parents.

Women bear the brunt of household tasks, and a man who helps around the house is a peculiar anomaly. Women tend to take pride in caring for their families, even forward-thinking, career-minded women. Foreign women who become romantically involved with Bosnian men will almost certainly have to discuss the sharing of household tasks with their partner, since they may not be used to the sort of  equitable distribution of chores that American or British women expect.

Gay or lesbian families are practically unheard of in BiH. While public opinion is slowly changing so that gay or lesbian couples are more accepted, this subject is generally not talked about. Public displays of affection between gay couples should be avoided, at least for now. There is general disapproval of the idea of gay or lesbian couples raising children. For the time being, most Bosnians feel that homosexuals should be free to love whomever they want, as long as they are discreet.

THE BOSNIAN HOME

Real estate prices, even in Sarajevo, are generally lower than in other parts of Europe. Keep in mind, however, that what is cheap to the foreign visitor can be quite expensive locally. Bosnians' homes tend to be built in the Mediterranean style, with white stucco walls and red-tiled roofs. Clothes are kept in armoires, or wardrobes—there are no built-in closets. The central room is usually a combined dining and living area, where families get together to eat, watch TV, or enjoy a cup of coffee. Most homes have one or two stories, and are quite spacious. Many also feature a small vegetable garden.

Children have their own rooms, and there will often be both a family room and a more formal receiving area. The kitchen is the center of family life. Homes are quite comfortable, but the cost can be prohibitive for the young or unemployed, so most people live with their parents well into adulthood. When they do buy their own place, it is often close to their parents or in-laws.

Private homes always have bathrooms with a toilet and a shower, and sometimes a bathtub. Some homes and apartments use water heaters to warm the water for the shower or bath; these must be turned on a good hour before you need it, and the hot water will run out after ten minutes or so. It's also environmentally friendly to "half-flush" the toilet when this is all that is necessary, simply by pressing the lever down halfway.

While most Bosnians live on meager incomes, there are a few very rich Bosnians living off bribes or mob money, or by skimming public coffers. Their homes are showy and glamorous, with gated yards, security cameras, and guard dogs. Very few people of wealth have obtained it through entirely honest means, so do be aware.

RENTING AN APARTMENT

If you intend to stay in Bosnia for an extended period of time, you'll probably find your living arrangements to be very comfortable. By American and European standards it tends to be quite cheap to rent an apartment—typically between 150 KM (about US $100 as of early 2009) per month for a normal one-bedroom place to around 400 KM (roughly US $270) per month for a luxury apartment in the center of town.

The best option for finding housing in Bosnia is to talk to friends or colleagues you already know in the country. At the very least, check with your embassy for recommendations of trusted landlords or real estate agents. Be careful before signing a contract for your new home, and read it thoroughly beforehand. Some landlords can be unreasonable, trying to charge much higher rents for foreigners or demanding that tenants move out at a few days' notice.

Landlords can be more involved in their

tenants' lives than foreigners are used to. New tenants will often be welcomed as honored guests, and treated accordingly. Some landlords may stop by frequently to chat or to check on the place. Depending on your preferences, this can be either hospitable or interfering. Try to set boundaries early if necessary. Keep in mind that such attention is kindly meant, and respond by inviting your new landlord over for coffee or dinner—on your schedule.

DAILY LIFE

Daily life can vary from family to family, depending on whether the parents are employed and whether the children are in school. The working week follows a predictable schedule. For most jobs, the adults are up and out of the house by 7:00 or 8:00 a.m. to reach the workplace by 9:00 a.m. Few families own more than one car, so public transportation in the cities is frequently used and walking is common in the small towns where everything is close together.

In the evenings, families eat together and rarely dine out during the week. On the weekends, however, it is common to go out for lunch, especially on Sundays. Friends will often get together for a barbecue or a picnic in the country. In the evenings, families may stroll outside together, especially along the Miljaska River in Sarajevo. The entire adjacent road closes at 5:00 p.m., in order to allow people to amble comfortably.

Young people go out to clubs, bars, or cinemas during the week. Cultural events, such as the theater and concerts, are popular in the towns and cities.

THE LOCAL MARKET

Most Bosnians typically go to their nearby corner shop for their grocery needs. If you're in Bosnia for any extended period of time, you'll probably become familiar with your local shops, which will generally have vegetables, fruit, dry pasta, milk, and basic toiletries. There are larger supermarkets in the bigger towns, but most packaging is not in English. Most areas also have a daily or weekly vegetable market that sells fresh produce. Bread can also be bought in small *pekaras* (bakeries).

There are certain foods that aren't common in Bosnia, or are difficult to find. In addition, some foods may be subtly different from what you're used to. Sugar tends to be coarser, and the finer, molasses-rich brown sugar that Americans use for baking is almost impossible to come by. Vanilla is sold in tiny glass vials and is much sweeter, so you might have to adjust your recipes. Basil and mint are nonexistent. You might also have to try specialty stores for items like chickpeas.

Don't worry too much about finding your favorite food or brand in Bosnia. Ninety percent of the time it, or an equivalent, will be available. As for the other 10 percent—welcome to Bosnia!

YOUNG PEOPLE

Bosnians love children, and dote on them affectionately. Children are a solid focal point of social gatherings and it is quite common for them to be brought along to parties, bars, and restaurants.

Bosnian parenting is both conservative and permissive. Often, parents do whatever they can to keep their children happy, and may appear overly permissive to foreigners. Even when families can't afford to give much to their children, they lavish them with attention and care.

Many Bosnians are in some way involved in looking after children aside from their own, including those of extended family and friends. As a result, they are used to giving their opinions on child care, and may readily offer you advice on your own parenting skills. Be prepared for comments about how warmly or otherwise your child is dressed, or to receive disdainful stares if you attempt to punish a child in public.

Parents are quite protective of their children, even as they mature. Most parents will not let their teenage or college-age children travel outside the country (assuming they can get the appropriate visas). Children remain close to their parents throughout their entire lives, and, as we have seen, will often live near them in adulthood. It is uncommon for young Bosnians to take a gap year or attend school abroad, not only because of the expense or bureaucracy involved, but also because they are a bit sheltered and may feel nervous about traveling so far on their own.

Children generally live with their parents until they are married. It's improper for two young people to visit each other at home, so often the parks will be filled with young couples necking.

Bosnian youth—teens and students—are like their counterparts everywhere. They love music, movies, going to clubs with their friends, and meeting for coffee. Some of the older ones have memories of the war, but they generally don't like to talk about politics and prefer to discuss their favorite bands or actors. This doesn't mean that they aren't informed or don't have opinions about political issues. Most speak English, and will be eager to practice their language skills with foreigners.

Most young Bosnians are more progressive than their parents and grandparents. While they are family oriented, with strong opinions or religious views, they generally tend to be tolerant and accepting of opposing viewpoints. This varies between the cities and the smaller towns. Religious views definitely have a bearing on opinions on controversial topics such as gay marriage and abortion, but most feel a distinction between their own views and what others do. For example, a girl who is strongly against abortion would probably not judge a friend who decides to have one. For all the talk of divisiveness, there is a strong attitude of "live and let live."

Young Bosnians tend to be rather realistic and even pessimistic. They know that a poor job market awaits them. They can be understandably unmotivated at times. Often, they have rather meager career and life goals compared to young people in other countries. Many idly dream of studying or traveling abroad in order to broaden their opportunities, yet at the same time many feel a strong connection to BiH and want to live here as adults.

Bosnian youth care for their aging parents and respect their elders. They invariably offer their seats to older adults, and take time to speak with elderly neighbors.

EDUCATION

Bosnian children begin kindergarten around age three. They start primary school at five or six, and attend for eight years. They then transfer to secondary schools that often specialize in a particular subject, such as medicine or the arts. There are several universities in Bosnia, and more and more young people are continuing their education.

Despite attempts to reform the system, Bosnian education remains antiquated and typical of post-Communist countries. Great emphasis is placed on hard facts and little on critical thinking or analysis. As a result, most Bosnian students, especially those at university, can spout hundreds of facts and quote a huge number of great thinkers. It is unusual, however, for students to speak up in class or express a personal opinion in front of their peers.

This trend is slowly changing, and the Bologna system is coming into effect, with mixed results. The Bologna system attempts to standardize higher education across Europe. Currently, higher degrees from Bosnian universities are not recognized outside the country. The effects of this transition are varied. While the system is slowly becoming more attentive to the needs of the individual student, it's also creating mass confusion. Many students who are just starting university don't know what degree they will receive upon graduating; while the system is in transition, it can be unclear whether the program they enrolled in will qualify them for a BA, an MA, or simply a certificate—it can even change midway through their university careers. Older teachers are reluctant to adopt new teaching methods. In general, the entire system lacks materials and organization, and there is a lot of discontent. The current system also makes it difficult for students to pass, yet at the same time provides dozens of second chances when students fail an exam or miss an entire semester of class. It is not a meritocracy.

On the bright side, there is an influx of new young teachers who are eager to make the system more accommodating to Western standards of education. Bosnian students are talented and bright, and have great potential. In the meantime, however, inquiries into a student's satisfaction with the educational system are likely to bring forth disgruntled sighs and loud criticism.

VETERANS

Not surprisingly, there are a great number of war veterans in BiH, and the subject of pensions for veterans is a hot topic. At the moment, most are not receiving a pension, which is especially troublesome, given the unemployment rate and the number of disabled veterans. Posttraumatic stress disorder and depression are issues for everyone, but especially for veterans. While many are proud of the fact that they fought, it is naturally a very sensitive topic. In general, Bosnians have great respect for their veterans and support regular, fair pensions, as well as special privileges for them. However, the system is poorly managed, and pensions are often late, inadequate, and unequally distributed. Aside from this, the definition of a veteran can be rather arbitrary, so the system is occasionally abused.

EMPLOYMENT

Unemployment is an enormous issue in BiH, and statistics show that nearly half of the population is unemployed at any one time. Unemployment benefits do exist, but bureaucracy and lack of public information make it difficult to access these funds.

Jobs with international companies and diplomatic missions are seen as highly desirable; they tend to be reasonably stable and the pay and working conditions are generally good. Jobs with banks are also highly sought after, and have a certain cachet. Strangely, jobs as doctors or veterinarians are not very well regarded, as they don't pay well, are hindered by bureaucracy, and have limited funds for new equipment.

There is an increasing number of well educated but unemployed young people in Bosnia, as higher education is relatively inexpensive but job availability is low. Teachers, translators, lawyers, and economists wait tables, clean houses, or are supported by their parents while they wait for a job that's suited to their skill level.

SMOKING

Bosnians smoke. A lot. Laughably, there is supposedly a national law that prohibits smoking in public places, but this is completely ignored. Most Bosnians know that Europeans and Americans do not smoke as much, and will probably comment if you do. There may be one or two restaurants advertised as nonsmoking, but even there they often allow it if you ask. You will see mothers smoking while holding infants, you will see street children as young as six smoking in the bus stations, and

you will constantly be surrounded by a thick fog of smoke in cafés, bars, and restaurants. Cigarettes are cheap, often only a few KM, and readily available at kiosks and grocery stores.

If you do not smoke, and smoke bothers you, your options are limited. Try to sit outside when possible, but this is of little help in the winter. It would be crass to ask your tablemates not to smoke, although they would probably comply— just don't expect a return invitation. Even in homes where the family members do not smoke, there will probably be ashtrays around for guests. You probably won't see many people smoking as they stroll down the street—smoking is a social activity, enjoyed with coffee or after a meal. For the dedicated nonsmoker, at least for the time being, you simply have to grin and bear it.

chapter six

TIME OUT

Leisure time is a hallmark of Bosnian culture. Typical of Mediterranean culture, Bosnians spend time every day with their family and friends, with long lunches and frequent coffee breaks. Most take an annual vacation to the coast in July or August, and business can be slow during these months. Leisure time is generally spent in groups, at a local café or bar, and foreigners are welcome to join their new friends in this sort of activity. The most important leisure activity is the daily coffee break—the day simply isn't complete without a cup or two, lingered over with friends.

CAFÉ CULTURE

Many Bosnians skip breakfast, or simply have a cup of coffee and a cigarette in the morning. If you need something more substantial, stop by a *pekara* (bakery) for some *kifla* (rolls) or a croissant. Settle into a café with a coffee, or try some *sok* (juice). The Bosnians do wonderful things with juice, and you can get freshly squeezed *narandža sok* (orange juice) in most cafés. It's also not uncommon to order a *sendvić* (sandwich) for breakfast; these usually come on sub rolls filled with tuna or meat and cheese. The typical toppings are *salata* (cabbage), *krastavci* (pickles), *paradajz* (tomatoes), and lots of *majoneza* (mayonnaise) and *kečap* (ketchup).

For lunch on the go, most Bosnians grab a *burek* (meat pie) or a *sendvič*. *Hamburger* or *pileći filet* (chicken sandwiches) are also common. One of the prides of Bosnian cuisine is *ćevapčići*—sausages and onions stuffed in soft bread called *somun*. There's great rivalry

among various *ćevapi* places, and especially among the regions. Make sure you say that you prefer the *ćevapi* from whatever town you're in!

Pizza is another popular fast-food item, although the crust is thinner than American pizza, and it rarely has much tomato sauce. Bosnians like to put ketchup on their pizza, but that can taste slightly different as well—it's often made with paprika or with a barbecue flavor.

Palančinka (crepes, essentially) can be either savory or sweet, and are a delicious alternative when you need a break from the ubiquitous *burek*. These can be filled with anything, but cheese and *gljieve* (mushrooms) are both popular. For dessert, try them filled with Nutella, *voće* (fruit), or *med* (honey). You could also stop by any of the numerous *slastičarnas* (sweet shops)—that is, if you haven't already been sucked in by the decadent displays of cake and *sladoled* (ice cream) in the window. Bosnians love cake and ice cream, and they do a marvelous job with them. Since the daily availability usually varies, it's perfectly acceptable to go to the display case and point to what you want before sitting down. If you're not quite sure, you can just specify what sort of mood you're in—chocolaty, fruity, hazelnutty, etc. At some point, do order *baklava,* (pronounced with the emphasis on the second syllable). This honey and nut-filled delicacy, a remnant of Bosnia's Ottoman past, is sweet, rich, and absolutely mouthwatering.

Most Bosnians also make a visit to a local *pekara* during the day to buy various pastries, pies, and bread. *Pitas* consist of phyllo dough stuffed with various fillings. *Burek* is the most common, and is stuffed with meat. *Sirnica,* with cheese, is also popular. Other varieties include *zeljanica* (spinach), *krompiruša* (potato), and *tikvanica* (squash). They're all delicious, and usually come with a side dish of *pavlaka,* a sort of yogurty cheese to smother on top. You simply haven't been to Bosnia unless you've tried one of these.

BOSNIAN CUISINE

Bosnian cuisine is rich, hearty, and meaty—
perfect for those cold, winter Bosnian days. If
you have the time, you should certainly have
a traditional, leisurely Bosnian meal.
Start out with an order of *uštipci*—
fried dough, served piping hot
with a side of *kajmak* (creamy,
buttery cheese) to spread on top.
You might want to follow up with
supa (soup). *Begova čorba* is a
traditional take on chicken soup, and is
filling and delicious. Tomato soup is commonly
on menus, but it's slightly different from
American-style tomato soup, and often bulked
out with rice. There is a huge variety of meat
dishes, including lamb, beef, chicken, and pork.
Most meat is locally raised and free of hormones
and other markers of industrial production. *Kebab*
(grilled meat on a stick) and *čorba* (stew) are
popular; *klepe* is a wonderfully delicious meat-
filled ravioli smothered in a creamy sauce. Fish is
also popular, and typically comes whole, with
head and skin.

Fine dining is Bosnia is certainly available, but
still isn't up to the standards of Western Europe
and abroad. Italy isn't far west of Bosnia, and
there is a long history of Italians coming to
Croatia (and, consequently, Bosnia) so their
culinary traditions have been adopted here to
some degree. All forms of pasta and various
sauces are easily available, at least in the larger

cities, and many of the good restaurants are Italian. Apart from Italian food, there are few options for other foreign cuisine.

For those with special dietary needs, Bosnia can be difficult. Vegetarians? There are plenty of fresh fruits and vegetables, and most are organic, by accident, if not by design. There are a great number of wonderful local cheeses as well. Vegans? Good luck!

DRINK

Bosnia, as we have seen, is a coffee culture, and the typical day includes coffee breaks with friends (see pages 83-84). In the summer, the cafés overflow on to the streets, with people sipping *kafa sa mlijekom*—a shot of strong coffee with milk—or "Nes." When it's hot, try the fruit juices. *Limunada* is a popular and refreshing drink—this is freshly squeezed, unsweetened lemon juice, served at room temperature with cane sugar on the side. In the cooler months, you

can warm up with a delicious *topla čokolada,* which is a thick, rich, hot chocolate drink.

Bosnia is full of natural lakes and rivers, and in consequence there is a big market for locally produced water, both still and sparkling. If you ask

for *voda* (water), you will probably be given a bottle. If you simply want tap water (which is perfectly safe to drink, and tastes quite wonderful), ask for a *čaša voda* (a glass of water). Ice is not commonly served with drinks in Bosnia, and serving sizes may be much smaller than you're used to, especially if you're American. Popular bottled waters include Sarajevkso or Kiseljak; if you want still water, ask for *voda bez gas.*

There are local wines, beers, and hard liquors that you should certainly sample if you choose. While most Bosnians are very proud of their local wines, they can be extremely tannic and acidic. If you want a draft beer, ask for a *točeno pivo.* Light beers are *svietlo.* Dark beer, or *tamno pivo,* are less common but, when available, are usually delicious.

Local brandies, or *rakia,* are fruit- or herb-based, and tend to be quite strong. It's common to order one after a big dinner, and it's definitely worth trying. The most common is *šljivovica,* made from plums.

NAVIGATING A RESTAURANT

When you arrive at a restaurant or café, seat yourself immediately, unless you want to check out the display case of cakes. If a waiter or waitress approaches you when you enter, especially at a nicer place, they may accompany you to a table, but you're expected to choose where you want to sit.

In bigger cities, most waiters and waitresses speak some English, and there may even be an English menu if you ask for it. Be prepared for certain items to be unavailable; much of the food is seasonal and local. As you order, your *račun* (bill) will be placed on the table. If you order at multiple points in the meal (for example, you start with drinks, then order the main course later, and finish up with dessert or coffee), you might have a wad of bills sitting on the table by the end.

If you have a special dietary need, or are hankering for something in particular, it's quite acceptable to ask for it. Particularly in smaller, family-owned restaurants, they're happy to accommodate you with something that's not on the menu. The service in these small family restaurants is generally quite good, but the waiters in cafés or city restaurants can be surly and reluctant. Don't take it personally; they are dismally paid and tipping isn't common.

When it's time to pay, hand the money directly to the person who served you. Don't leave money on the table, or it may disappear before your server has a chance to pick it up. You can get up and find the waiter if you're in a hurry. Sometimes a waiter or waitress may approach you before you have finished your meal, asking you to pay the bill; this means their shift is over and they need to settle their outstanding orders.

Most Bosnians do not take food out of restaurants (doggy bags). However, if you ask, the waiters will generally be happy to wrap up whatever you want. Don't be shy; they probably have already figured out you're a foreigner by this point.

TIPPING

Most Bosnians do not tip, or they simply round the bill up to the nearest KM. If you're feeling generous in a café or casual restaurant, 10 to 15 percent is generally more than enough for a tip. In better restaurants, tip according to the service you receive; 15 to 20 percent is more common in these places.

For those providing services other than food, such as taxi drivers or hairdressers, you are not expected to tip. You'll certainly make a good impression, however, if you do. Remember that the economy in Bosnia is very poor, and most people struggle to make ends meet. A few extra KM are very much appreciated.

VISITING A MOSQUE

On your first morning in Bosnia you'll probably
be woken by the dawn call to prayer. This can be
unwelcome at 5:00 a.m. when you're suffering
from jet lag, but it can also be a lovely reminder
of the unique history of Bosnia.

Many of the mosques in Bosnia are quite
beautiful and well maintained, as the Islamic
community is large and well managed. Avoid
visiting a mosque during main prayer hours. In
the cities, some of the larger mosques offer tours.
Come prepared by being modestly dressed. That
means covered legs (no shorts), and long sleeves.
Many mosques offer scarves for women to cover
their heads, but bring your own just in case. If
you are not Muslim, it is perfectly acceptable
simply to drape the scarf over your hair rather
than cover it completely. Take your shoes off and
leave them by the door before entering the main
prayer area. You will probably see people
washing their hands and feet in a fountain near
the entrance; this is a preparatory ritual for
prayer, and it's not necessary for visitors to
follow suit. Turn off your cell phone, and remain
quiet. Be respectful of anyone who is praying in
the mosque. Some mosques are more
conservative than others—be aware if men and
women are clearly going into separate entrances.
If you aren't sure about anything, just ask.

If you have never visited a mosque before, you
might be nervous about offending someone or

doing something "wrong." Don't let this deter you from visiting. Bosnians are extremely welcoming and willing to share their culture, and are very understanding of those who aren't familiar with Islamic customs.

MONEY

The Bosnian Convertible Mark (BAM) is generally referred to as KM in day-to-day conversation. "Cents" are called *feniks* (from the German "*Pfennig*"). Bosnia's is primarily a cash economy, although credit and debit cards are accepted in some restaurants and hotels. Be sure to withdraw the money that you are likely to need before traveling to small towns, as ATMs can be difficult to find. Euros are accepted almost everywhere in Sarajevo, but it's best not to rely on this.

It is useful to know how to say numbers in Bosnian, and they aren't difficult to remember. The "teens" are formed by adding "-*naest*" to the basic numbers (*trinaest*, *petnaest*, and so on). The "twenties" are formed by preceding each number with "*dvadeset*" (*dvadeset dva*, *dvadeset tri*). The convention follows for everything higher (*trideset*, *cetirideset*, and so on). Knowing the numbers will help you in the marketplace and keep you from blindly handing a cashier a wad of bills without knowing how much change to expect.

1 *jedan* (pronounced "yay-dan")
2 *dva*
3 *tri* ("tree")
4 *četiri* ("che-ter-i")
5 *pet* ("payt")
6 *šest* ("shayst")
7 *sedam* ("say-dam")
8 *osam*
9 *devet*
10 *deset* ("de-cet")

A common money word is *polje,* which means "half." Cashiers will ask for *"polje marke,"* half a mark, rather than *petdeset feniks.* Remember to carry small bills and coins. If a cashier or taxi driver doesn't have change for larger denominations (and they often won't), you're out of luck. It can be difficult to find a place to exchange larger bills for smaller ones. You can go to a bank, or ask in one of the larger shops or restaurants. A good hotel may also help you out, but at any of these places, they'd be doing you a favor and might refuse. Even if you're a legitimate customer, they may still grumble when you hand them a 100 KM bill.

SHOPPING
There is a rich tradition of handicraft in Bosnia, and there are many opportunities to buy excellent metalwork, jewelry, rugs, and other handmade items. In the old towns of Sarajevo, Travnik,

Mostar, and Banja Luka, you can buy crafted items for good prices. There really are some beautiful pieces of work here, and most are unique to Balkan culture.

Western goods aren't available for much lower prices in Bosnia than they would be elsewhere. The exceptions are CDs, DVDs, and cigarettes. The black market for pirated CDs and DVDs is thriving, and they tend to be pretty good quality. You can find practically every major artist or movie title, and the shops run in broad daylight in fixed locations. Since there are few legitimate stores where CDs and DVDs are sold legally, many Bosnians buy goods at the "market." Cigarettes are also extremely cheap, costing between 1.5 KM and 4 KM a pack.

Bosnians generally do not haggle. In the vegetable markets or in small shops, it may be possible to try for a deal, but most salesclerks will resist it. If there is a visible price tag on an item, bargaining should not be attempted. Most shops try to keep prices fairly consistent between them, which is why haggling doesn't generally work. Quality can vary a lot, however, especially for tourist items, so focus on this. It is better to shop around for the best quality rather than the best price.

Strays
When you're out shopping, you will see many stray dogs and cats wandering the streets. There are no public services to manage this issue, and stray animals wander all over the country, but they tend to be quite tame, and rabies isn't a major concern. You will often see stray animals foraging for food in dumpsters, and Bosnians are sympathetic to the animals in a way that some foreigners might find strange. It's common to feed strays, and even to pet them. Many people get their pets from the streets rather than from pet stores. Keep your distance, and don't be frightened if you see a pack of dogs roaming the city. Above all, don't add to the stray animal problem by abandoning a short-term pet. If you do adopt an animal in the short term, there are many ways to ensure that it finds a good home; check with your embassy for options. If you're interested in helping, there are several animal rescue programs that find homes for the animals in Austria, Germany, and other European countries.

As a cultural note, there is some aversion to dogs in Islamic culture. While there are no prohibitions in the Koran against dogs, cultural and legal treatises in Islam consider them to be impure.

SPORTS

Watching sports is extremely popular in Bosnia, especially soccer (football). Local matches have large turnouts, and betting shops are often full of hopeful men. There is reported to be some degree of corruption or "fixing" in the local matches, so do be careful if you choose to bet. In addition, the rivalries between local teams can be fierce and the trash talk can quickly become personal. It is sad, but not uncommon, to hear even young children using ethnic slurs to refer to the opposing team.

Popular sports among youth, especially boys, include soccer, basketball, and handball. There aren't many youth leagues, however, and most girls don't play sports. Parks are lacking or poorly maintained. There are fitness clubs in some cities with aerobic equipment, free weights, and aerobics classes, but these can be difficult to find and aren't up to the standard of the rest of Europe.

Jogging is not a popular sport in Bosnia, and it can be difficult to find good places to run. If you go for a jog, you almost immediately mark yourself as a foreigner, especially if you are a woman. As always, be wary of running on unpaved areas since there are still land mines in some parts of Bosnia. Running in town can likewise be dangerous—the sidewalks are few and cars often commandeer them to park. Be very careful of traffic if you choose to jog; this is *not* a pedestrian-friendly country.

A great way to meet locals and other expats is to join the Sarajevo Hash House Harriers for a weekly jog and drinking session. The Hash is a worldwide running club with groups in most countries. While the format varies from country to country, it's all based on the idea of a casual run followed by socializing afterward. It's a wonderful way to meet people in a new place, especially if you're a frequent traveler. Don't worry if you're not a big runner—there are walking groups, and the trails change every week, so it's a great way to familiarize yourself with the city too.

NIGHTLIFE

Nightlife in Bosnia varies from town to town, but it's never difficult to find a bar, no matter where you are. Drinks are inexpensive, especially beer. Domestic beers are most common, and vary according to location—Sarajevsko in Sarajevo, Nektar in Banja Luka, and Tuzlanska in Tuzla—but imported beers are sometimes available. The Bosnian nightlife is dominated by youth, as is expected, but adults are certainly in the bar scene.

Most dance clubs will be packed to bursting with young people dancing, smoking, and drinking. If you just want a quiet drink, you're better off in a café than a bar. Most places will have live music on weekends, but beware of the dreaded "*technofolk.*"

This type of music is unique to Bosnia, and combines traditional folk music with techno beats. Some people love it, but many Bosnian youth scorn it, especially in the cities.

The music scene tends to be locally based, and the musical style of the area has commonly developed from folk melodies or stories, with lyrical melody lines and simple instrumental accompaniment. A popular local band is Erogene Zone, which combines traditional style with pop/rock elements. Concerts in the area are very low priced and most CDs are purchased illegally, so musicians

are forced to have day jobs, even if they're extremely popular. Bosnians view rock stars

differently from fans in some other countries.
It varies from disdain (how dare you be
successful in this country!) to relaxed admiration
(he's talented, but he's still just a regular guy).
You won't see people rushing to take photos of
celebrities or asking for autographs.

CULTURAL ACTIVITIES

There is a rich cultural life throughout Bosnia,
especially in Sarajevo. Numerous festivals that

draw international
attention are held
throughout the
year. Major events
include the
Sarajevo Film
Festival, the
MESS Theater
Festival, wine
festivals, and several other musical and dramatic
events. The arts are truly thriving in Bosnia, and
the quality of the productions equals anything
you would find in Europe or America.

OUTDOOR ACTIVITIES

There are many opportunities to enjoy outdoor
life in Bosnia, and this sector of tourism is more
developed than others. There are several hiking
companies, notably Green Visions, based in
Sarajevo. Trips to mountain villages, waterfalls,

and national parks are popular, and shouldn't be missed. While there are some local hiking groups, this is mostly a tourist activity. In addition to hiking, rafting companies coordinate trips down several rivers in Bosnia, including the Neretva and the Una. Skiing is a popular winter

sport, and Bjelsnica, Igman, and Jahorina are great places to start. The 1984 Winter Olympics were held here, but services are sometimes not up to the standard of skiing in the rest of Europe or America.

Use common sense when exploring the outdoors, and stick to areas that have obviously had recent human traffic. Up to a million land mines still remain in the countryside, so exercise caution before exploring on your own.

chapter seven

TRAVELING

Traveling in Bosnia can be somewhat of a
harrowing experience. The bus and train stations
are run-down, dirty, and have few English-
speaking ticket agents. The roads are generally of
poor quality, so bus and car travel can take hours.
Despite these flaws, public transportation is
reliable, cheap, and safe. People frequently use
the bus and train systems to visit family or even
to commute to work, but the buses and trains
aren't generally very crowded. The travel
experience in Bosnia isn't exactly pleasant, but it
is predictable once you get the hang of things.

ENTERING BOSNIA

Options for reaching BiH are relatively limited,
especially by air. The country still attracts few
tourists, so most travel information is in the local
language and requires some scouting.

By air, there are several routine flights into the
country, all flying into Sarajevo. Dulles
International is the main US hub. British Airways
also offers indirect flights to Sarajevo. There are
airports in Banja Luka and Mostar, but these are

much smaller and offer few international flights. The main stopover points in Europe are Munich and Vienna; there are also direct flights to Istanbul, Zagreb, Belgrade, and Munich; flights to other European cities may also be available. Upon landing, you will probably be given a landing card to fill out and you will be asked to keep it to turn in upon your departure. Rarely do they actually ask for this to be returned. From the airport, it is best to take a cab into the city. The fare should be about 15 KM—don't let the cabdrivers overcharge you just because you're a foreigner. There are also rental car agencies at the airport, though renting cars in Bosnia tends to be quite expensive. Taxis are cheap, ubiquitous, and safe.

Be sure to have a valid passport when entering the country. Americans, Canadians, and EU citizens do not need a visa. Visitors from other countries should check with their local Bosnian Embassy about specific requirements. Entering the country automatically grants the visitor a ninety-day visa. Those who plan to stay longer than ninety days should plan on leaving the country and reentering before this deadline in order to begin a new ninety-day period, even though this is rarely enforced. Those who plan to live or work in BiH are supposed to apply for a resident's permit; this is an incredibly lengthy process and most policemen will encourage you simply to leave and reenter the country every ninety days. Upon entering the country, you should register with the local police within forty-eight hours, although there is really no way to enforce this. Anyone who remains in the country for business purposes should obtain a business visa.

Border controls are standardized and are generally very quick and easy. Some guards with a machismo attitude might try to charge foreigners "special fees." You can pay to end it quickly, or argue and demand a receipt—this usually ends the discussion. Customs into and out of the country are lax, but technically follow standard European limits on duty-free goods. Passengers are sometimes known to distribute cartons of cigarettes or the like temporarily among fellow travelers while passing through border crossings.

ROADS AND TRAFFIC

Driving in Bosnia can be rather alarming. To date, there are only fourteen miles (23 km) or so of highway in the country, although they are working to add more, at the rate of half a mile or so a year. Only half of the 13,700 miles (22,000 km) of road are paved. Most of the roads outside the cities are curving, narrow, and lack guardrails. Driving conditions can be bad in the mountains due to rain, snow, or fog. Drivers share the road with heavy trucks, and there is rarely lighting outside the cities. The speed limit is 60 kmph (37 mph) and sometimes 80 kmph (50 mph)—speed limit signs are rare, so err on the side of caution.

The unspoken rules of the road are generally aggressive. Expect to be passed on harrowing, one-lane mountain curves. Bosnian drivers will speed in front of you but suddenly slam on their brakes for every bump or curve of the road— maybe because of the poor suspension on the ubiquitous fifteen-year-old Jugos. Drivers will cut you off, swerve across three lanes of traffic, honk mercilessly, and expect you to get out of their way. There is little parking in the city, so cars often park on the sidewalks. Rights of way are optional, so be very careful at intersections. It is best simply to be aware of drivers around you and to expect the unexpected.

One amusing and often frustrating quirk of Bosnian driving is the magical power of the blinker. Bosnians will stop in the middle of the road and flip on their hazard lights to chat with someone they know on the road or in an oncoming car. There is no use in honking at them—you simply have to wait.

Renting cars can be expensive, especially if you don't drive a stick shift. Gas is also much more expensive than in America. Make sure you have a valid driver's license, and insurance and registration documents if you bring your own car. Wearing seat belts is mandatory and talking on cell phones while driving is illegal, although most Bosnians break both these laws regularly. The legal Blood Alcohol Content is .05 percent.

Around Sarajevo, you will see many cars with black license plates and yellow lettering; these are cars with diplomatic immunity. If you drive one of these cars, please be aware that everyone knows you are a foreigner and respect the local traffic laws. In any case, never leave anything valuable in your car, as it will probably not be there when you return—and nor will the windows. Flashy or expensive cars are targeted for break-ins.

If a policeman flags you down while holding a round sign, you must pull over. He will probably attempt to give you a ticket for a fine, which shouldn't exceed 30 KM. Play the dumb foreigner card and you should be able to get out of it—the policeman is probably only trying to make a few extra bucks.

LOCAL TRANSPORTATION
Taxis
Even with the recent increase in base taxi fares, cabs are a cheap and easy way to get around if you don't know where you're going. You can hail one simply by raising your arm to an approaching taxi, or you can find one of the many taxi stands

throughout the cities. You can also call a cab by dialing 1515 on your phone. Cabdrivers rarely speak English, so it's a good idea to write down the address of where you want to go. There is no need to tip, but it is general practice to round the bill up to the next KM. Even though the ATMs rarely give out small bills, try to have small money on hand as most drivers have difficulty giving change. Taxis can also be hired for regular service. The following simple words can make the ride go more smoothly: *ovdje* ("ohv-dya," "here," to indicate that the driver should stop now); *pravo* ("straight," meaning "keep going"); *lijevo* ("li-yevo," "left"); *desno* ("right").

Trams

Sarajevo is currently the only part of the country with a functioning tram (streetcar) system, and it is widely used and reliable. However, the trams tend to be packed, and pickpocketing is common. The fare for a tram ride is 1.20 KM, and exact money is recommended. Tickets can be bought on board or at kiosks; after boarding, you must punch your ticket in the machine. You can ask the driver or other passengers when to get off, but they may not speak English.

The trams are regularly policed and they will ask to see your ticket. If you do not have one, you will be asked to pay a fine, generally around 30 KM. Some police may cut you a break for being a foreigner; others will harass you and try to get more money out of you.

Many of the trams were donated by foreign governments, so it is not unusual to see Japanese or German flags painted on the outside. Most are rather dilapidated, and there is little money to improve the system. While some locals try to avoid paying fares, it is not recommended for visitors to attempt this.

Buses

Bus travel is the most popular way to get around Bosnia and abroad. Intercity buses run frequently, are quite inexpensive, very punctual, and not usually very crowded. They tend to be a bit slow, however. On longer trips, buses will break about every two hours at a café or restaurant so that people can have a coffee, smoke a cigarette, or use the bathroom.

Bus travel is actually quicker than train travel in Bosnia, and there are several international lines that make regular stops throughout the country. Centrotrans is the main operator.

Bus stations are dirty and dilapidated. There is rarely a comfortable (or clean) place to wait, and Roma children prowl through asking for money. Credit or debit cards are not accepted and it's not uncommon for ATMs to be out of service, if they are there at all. The bathrooms often require a fee of 1 KM, and the interiors are smelly and flooded, with no toilet paper and often just a squat toilet (hole in the floor). Only rarely do the ticket clerks or bus drivers speak English. In other words, a horrible bus station experience is practically a rite of passage for foreigners. However, while it may take a few attempts to get used to the system, buses are probably the best way to get around the country.

Trains
The trains do not run frequently as the rail system was badly damaged during the war and has not recovered. Trains also tend to take longer than bus travel. There are several train routes in and out of the country, including Sarajevo from Ploče, on the Dalmatian coast, from Zagreb, and from Budapest. Trains are useful if the bus schedule doesn't suit your needs.

Walking
Pedestrians do not have the right of way in Bosnia, so be extremely cautious when crossing the street. Pay attention to the crossing indicators and do not attempt to jaywalk or to dash across at the end of a pedestrian signal—the cars won't wait for you to finish. Always stay on paved roads, and be mindful of signs for land mines.

WHERE TO STAY
The options for accommodation are rather limited. The best hotels are in Sarajevo, including

the famous Holiday Inn. This was a hot spot of journalists during the war, and was badly damaged. Its bright yellow facade is a landmark in the city. Several other (expensive) hotels are available. Outside the capital there are few four-star options. Most travelers in Bosnia are diplomats or aid workers, who stay mainly in the capital and have cash to burn; the hospitality industry quickly adapted to accommodate them.

There are a number of reasonably priced hotels and hostels in larger cities, but don't expect the same amenities. Most small places are family affairs with a cozy charm. Hostels are popular with budget-conscious travelers and are available in the larger cities, with accommodation ranging from dormitories to rooms in private homes. Even in these less expensive options you will find typical Bosnian hospitality. To find accommodation, you can try Internet listings, but these may be limited outside Sarajevo.

APPLIANCES

Bosnia uses the regular European-style plugs
(Europlug or Schuko); they are either two-
pronged or three-pronged, and fit into recessed
plug outlets. American and British plugs will not
fit these outlets. You can buy plug adapters and
use many American or British appliances with
adapters. The voltage in Bosnia is 220 to 240
volts alternating at 50 cycles per second, while
American and Canadian appliances run at 110 to
120 volts. These kinds of appliances will require
both a plug adapter and a step-down transformer.
You can buy small, light, resistance-network
converters, but these can only be used for a short
period of time. Transformers are much bigger and
heavier, but can be used for extended periods.

To check the voltage of an appliance, look at
the label on the battery pack or plug; it should say
something like "Input: ~100-240V 50/60Hz
65W" (this is the sort of label on a multi-voltage
appliance that only needs a plug adapter) or
"Input: 120V 60Hz 2.8A" (for an appliance that
only runs on 120 volts and requires a transformer
or voltage adapter). Be careful to check your
appliances before plugging them in. Without the
proper voltage adapter, you could fry the
appliance or even start a fire.

For a short stay, converters will be sufficient
for your hair dryer or electric shaver. If you will
be in the country for any extended period of time,
it's advisable just to buy a few basic Bosnian
appliances (iron, vacuum cleaner, kettle) rather

than fiddle with adapters. These are not expensive, and it will be much more convenient. Transformers are useful for more expensive appliances you may not want to replace, such as TVs or microwaves. For really big appliances, such as refrigerators or washer dryers, you should hire an electrician. Note that taking TVs or other AV equipment abroad can be very troublesome, as most are made to be used locally in order to prevent piracy. If you wish to do this, get specialist advice.

Note that most laptops and other digital devices (such as cameras, cell phone chargers, and music players) are multi-voltage and only require a plug adapter. Desktop computers usually have a small switch near the cooling fan that allows them to switch from 120V to 220V, and will only need a plug adapter as long as the switch is in the right place.

If you are looking for plug adapters, buy "type c" for European CEE 7/16 Europlug or "type E/F" for European CEE 7/4 or CEE 7/5 Schuko.

HEALTH

Health services in Bosnia are improving, but still do not meet the standards of the rest of Europe or America. There is a lack of funding and coordination between health care facilities. Doctors are extremely dedicated and well trained, but are forced to work under difficult conditions. Bosnians generally have negative feelings about their health care system, and experience great difficulty in having their needs met. The clinics are often crowded and lack equipment, requiring long waits. Because of the entity divisions, individuals may have trouble accessing health care away from their place of residence. Foreigners generally go to the VIP clinic at the main hospital in Sarajevo; it costs a few extra KM but you are then forwarded to the front of the line. The hospitals and clinics are often a bit dilapidated and the equipment is generally not quite up-to-date. Despite the appearance of the health care facilities, the quality of care isn't much below European or American standards, at least for minor issues.

There are no required vaccinations to enter Bosnia, but most recommend getting vaccinated for hepatitis A and B, typhoid, tetanus-diphtheria, measles, chickenpox, and influenza. Travelers should also have a good health insurance policy that covers evacuation in the case of serious illness. Medications in Bosnia may not be the same brands as you are used to, so it is wise to bring your own supply of prescriptions and other such supplies to last for the duration of your stay. Certain drug store items may be more expensive or impossible to find. Contact lens solution is especially expensive. Women will be able to find tampons and sanitary napkins, but if you have a strong preference for a particular brand, bring your own supply.

It can be difficult to find doctors who speak English, especially outside Sarajevo. Your local embassy should have a list of doctors who speak other languages, but this does not mean that their command of English will be perfect. Many doctors make house calls, although this can be expensive. Bosnian doctors are more than capable of handling minor illnesses, but it is best to seek care outside Bosnia if a serious problem occurs.

SAFETY

In general, Bosnia is a safe place to visit. On the whole, crime rates are low and foreigners rarely have problems. There are, however, two special items of concern—theft and land mines—that should be mentioned.

Theft is not uncommon, but generally only takes place if the opportunity is there. Keep purses and laptops under close watch, and be on the lookout for pickpockets. As in any city, be aware of your surroundings, keep an eye on your belongings, and don't give potential thieves the opportunity. Thieves target foreigners because they often carry a lot of cash and they tend to get distracted. Avoid driving flashy cars or displaying cash openly, or you could be targeted. Organized crime does exist, and there are instances of random violence—be aware, avoid dark streets, and trust your instincts. Violent crime is rare, and when it does occur, it nearly always occurs when warring mafia groups target one another.

Land mines are a serious issue, but are easily avoided. During the war, a great number of mines were placed all over the country with little or no tracking system. Rural farmers would surround their property with land mines, and later forget

exactly where they put them. A great deal has
been done to remove the threat of land mines, but
it is impossible to know just
how much more needs to be
done. Always stay on paved
roads and do not walk in the
countryside unless
accompanied by a guide.
Avoid abandoned buildings
and open fields. Watch out

for signs for mines, but understand also that signs
are not always posted where mines might be.

Political unrest occurs occasionally, but is
limited in scope. Always check for the latest
travel warnings with your local embassy, and
avoid rallies or protests. It is wise to register with
your local embassy for the duration of your visit
and to know the emergency numbers for your
embassy in the case of an emergency.

Female visitors may be offended or pleased by
the sometimes blatant expressions of admiration
from strange men. If this attention truly bothers
you, consider wearing a wedding ring or try to
walk with male friends. Attention of this nature is
rarely dangerous or intended to insult, but trust
your instincts in any particular situation. Follow
the same kinds of rules as you would in any
major city: don't walk home alone late at night,
avoid alleys and talking on your phone, and
always have money for a cab if you feel unsafe.

chapter eight

BUSINESS BRIEFING

The legacy of Communism is probably most strongly felt in the business world of Bosnia–Herzegovina. A strong, patriarchal system, heavy

bureaucracy, and fledgling capitalism still hinder economic progress as the country shifts from a planned economy to a market-oriented one. While several broad statements about business in Bosnia can be made, there are some differences among the business cultures of certain ethnicities and among the various sectors. To do business successfully, you should learn as much as possible about the company you are to do business with, about the power structure within it, and about the way business has been done in the past with that company.

Many sectors of the Bosnian economy are now being privatized, with mixed feelings on the part of the locals. Capitalism changes not only the way business is done, but also the way people live their lives. Public-sector jobs may pay less, but offer long-term stability, guaranteed vacations, and fixed hours. Public-sector jobs are overstaffed and static, and unable to respond to changes in the market; reforms in this area, however, would add to the already enormous number of unemployed.

Jobs in the private sector generally operate on short-term contracts, have few protections for workers' rights, and require longer working hours. Bosnians want to embrace capitalism, but at the same time they resist how it changes their daily lives. There is no doubt that they will continue to make progress in this area as they push for EU candidacy, as a strong private sector is a requirement for EU membership in accordance with the Copenhagen criteria.

Unemployment is a major issue in the country, and for people who have work, job satisfaction tends to be low. They may endure poor working conditions simply for the paycheck, meager as it might be. Young people don't dream of the perfect job, but rather of whatever job they can get. Although wages are low, the cost of living is still high in comparison to other countries in the region, so paychecks must stretch very far. Some private businesses take advantage of the vulnerabilities of the Bosnian workforce, and there are few effective governmental checks on their behavior. As a result of these issues, illegal employment and the gray market have become major forces within the Bosnian economy to make up for deficiencies in salary.

The Bosnian economy is primarily service-based, but with a large sector involved in industry, too. Aid projects and international support greatly inflate the economy. The working week is strictly Monday to Friday, and the day

starts at 8:00 or 8:30 a.m. Offices generally stay open until 5:00 p.m., but retail stores tend to stay open several hours later. Banks are open until 6:00 p.m., but are closed on weekends. Some stores may close for midday breaks, but this is not common in Sarajevo.

Certain governmental and judicial reforms must take place before Bosnia can compete effectively on an international scale. While some laws are being passed that make it easier to conduct business in the country, they still have a long way to go. Statistics show that bureaucracy is a major hindrance to economic development. Bosnia is ranked 105 in terms of ease of doing business by the World Bank (of 178 ranked), and 150 for both dealing with licenses and starting a business. It can take literally years for a business to get up and running—setting up property or enforcing contracts can require dozens of procedures that move along at a snail's pace. See the World Bank's in-depth report *Doing Business in Bosnia Herzegovina* for an outline of the steps required for specific business procedures.

INTERCULTURAL COOPERATION

There are two main kinds of international business in Bosnia: foreign-owned private companies, and those established and run by international institutions, such as the Office of the High Representative (OHR), USAID, local embassies, and the Organization for Security and Co-operation in Europe (OSCE). Bosnians hired by either of these types of organizations experience fairer working conditions, better social services (like health care and retirement funds), and higher and more regular pay, but the political nature of international institutions raises important issues of their own. Despite the benefits of such jobs, some Bosnians are reluctant to accept them; while they appreciate the perks, they'd rather be running the show themselves. Perhaps the history of foreign involvement in the area causes some Bosnian businesspersons to resist foreign directives, but it is also true that many Bosnians are showing initiative and a desire for self-management. These reservations generally disappear as Bosnians work with international colleagues, especially if their colleagues are good bosses and do not act in a superior manner. The fact that international organizations pay on time is a huge selling point for Bosnians, and this does much to build trust and cooperation between local and international colleagues.

PERSONAL CONTACTS

The weight of personal relationships cannot be overstated. A close personal contact is tantamount to a successful deal—much more so than in other parts of the world. Bosnians rely heavily on personal contacts also to secure employment. In the public sector, an individual requires several connections to find a job, unless he or she has a close relation who is high up in the hierarchy. In the private sector, personal recommendations for jobs are less common, but come with their own set of rules. Individuals who are hired on the basis of recommendation are expected to work especially hard to prove their worth to the company and to their external contact.

Building a social relationship with employees can help you get your foot in the door. Seek out private contacts, and try to attend parties or dinners that the decision makers might attend.

BUSINESS DRESS

Business dress is similar to Western European and American standards of dress, but personal appearance carries an especially high premium in

Bosnia. Men wear conservative suits and ties to most business functions, and women wear dresses or skirts with stockings, generally opaque, and close-toed shoes. Well-fitting suits and fashionable accessories, including watches, bags, and scarves, will make a good impression. Few women wear slacks to the office, although it is by no means taboo. Be sure to include a dressy coat if you visit in winter. The Sarajevo streets can also be very, very slippery in winter and when it rains, so avoid high heels. Seriously. The embarrassment of falling over, while wearing a skirt, in front of a mosque full of men at prayer time has convinced most Bosnian women to save the heels for special, non-rainy occasions only.

Out of the office, dress is less formal and may include just slacks and sports coat. Women should dress fashionably, but avoid revealing outfits (even if you see them on women around you). While many Bosnians, especially the young, are less formal, it is impossible to predict how your personal business contacts will view such dress. It's better to play it safe.

POWER STRUCTURES

Who holds the power in any particular organization may not always be self-evident. While some businesses, especially those run by Serb or Muslim men, have strong, top-down decision-making processes, others may operate in a more consensual way. In addition, it may not always be clear who the key figure is, and it is best simply to ask who's in charge. Status counts for much, and skipping the chain of command could sour a business deal from the beginning.

To get off on the right foot, find out who is in charge before you set up a meeting. In private business, go to the very top of the chain of command to begin with. Find out the person's complete job title (Executive Director or Chief of Operations), and "drop" the title followed by their full name throughout your interactions. Make sure that you spell the person's name correctly, and learn how to pronounce the name before the meeting.

In the public sector, job mobility or advancement is difficult to come by, unless your immediate supervisor retires or dies. In the private sector, things are little more fluid and most workers expect to move up during their career. A promotion is a big deal for people, as they happen so rarely, which is one of the reasons job titles matter so much.

ARRANGING A MEETING

Once you've figured out whom you need to speak to, it can be difficult to arrange a meeting with that person. Government officials are especially difficult to pin down. E-mail is generally not a reliable way to contact new colleagues—some people don't check their e-mails regularly—so the telephone is a much more effective way to do so. If you are really struggling to find contacts, it is acceptable simply to show up. This may well be the easiest and quickest way to get in the door.

Bosnians work hard, but they like to go home at the end of the day to their families and tend not to work past 4:00 or 5:00 p.m. Schedule meetings for the morning to ensure a timely reception, and avoid scheduling meetings on Friday afternoons or during July and August, when many people are on vacation.

MEETINGS

In the meeting itself, be prepared to use a translator. While basic English will probably be spoken, most Bosnians cannot speak it well enough to hold a full business conversation. German is widely spoken among successful Bosnian businessmen. During the meeting, your Bosnian colleagues are likely to remain quiet and respectful, asking few questions. The chain of command is important; while you speak, remember to direct yourself primarily to the person in charge. Keep presentations short, dynamic, and to the point. Bosnians will be judging your personality as much as your proposal, so make the presentation interesting, with slides, anecdotes, jokes, or illustrative case studies. Call ahead to see what kind of technical equipment is available, and have a backup plan in case there is a problem. Even so, a last-minute change of room (certainly not unheard of) could mean that your carefully planned PowerPoint presentation cannot be used. During the meeting, be sure to drop a few key phrases, like "European success," "highest standards of quality," or "investment in your company." These will jump-start negotiations considerably.

Meetings may take place in the office or, occasionally, in a café. In keeping with the importance of personal relationships, it is common for business to be done over lunch, and this signals confidence in your proposal. These lunch meetings can take a while, so be sure to schedule enough time for a leisurely meal. Eat heartily and show respect for the culture by drinking coffee and eating Bosnian foods. Often, these meetings are accompanied with several shots of *rakia*, a fruit brandy. It is acceptable to sip these slowly, which might be wise under business circumstances. Take advantage of the situation to bond with your colleagues in a nonbusiness conversation. Football is an especially popular topic, and one that maintains the general machismo that often pervades these meetings.

For these sorts of personal meetings, it might be appropriate to bring a small gift for your hosts. This is certainly not expected, but can help to foster the relationship. Make sure the gifts are modest so that they cannot be construed as a bribe. Items with your company logo, some liquor from home, or business items, such as pens or calendars, would be appropriate choices.

PUNCTUALITY

Bosnians in general operate on a more relaxed schedule, and deadlines tend to be fluid. It is not unusual to be kept waiting for meetings, either at the office or with friends. As the Western business approach becomes stronger in the region, however, this is changing. In addition, it is a mark of respect to show up on time, especially for personal functions like dinner at someone's home. As many important meetings might take place in a restaurant or café, a few minutes' tardiness should be expected, but avoided. There is a slight double standard; internationals are expected to be prompt, but Bosnians are more likely to be late. Certainly, there are some interesting psychological power plays fueling this standard.

NEGOTIATING WITH BOSNIANS

While most Bosnians are honest, corruption and fraud does exist and there are few avenues to pursue if contracts are broken or if money is misappropriated. Protect your investments by thoroughly investigating the company you plan to work with before signing anything or handing money over. Transfer money in small increments based on the performance of the company, and keep money out of local banks until necessary, although the banks in Bosnia are becoming more secure every day. Also, apprise yourself of the proper contracts and permits that must be signed.

Bosnians like to ponder a proposal and will probably need some time before making a decision. It is useful to put everything in writing, and specify who will be responsible for enforcing the contract. Local courts can be very tedious and expensive, so international courts may offer more reassurance. Smaller contracts, like those for employment or internal state affairs, will generally only need to be notarized by the local courts. For larger and more expensive contracts, such as those involving imports or exports, it may be wise to use international courts (outline as such in the contract). Bosnians will generally uphold the terms of a contract, as long as it is official, but delays in fulfilling the terms may occur due to the overwhelming bureaucracy in the country.

GREASING THE WHEELS

Bribery is still an issue, especially when trying to get permits approved. Local governments often require an unofficial "going rate" for certain services, and this does not necessarily lead to preferential treatment—just treatment. The cooperation of the local government is a necessary part of doing business, so bribery may be impossible to avoid and is better considered as a fee-for-service. Small bribes to clerks still occur, but are declining in frequency. Large bribes should not be attempted, although they certainly happen between politicians and criminals (considered to be the same thing by many Bosnians).

Using the terms "bribe" and "fraud" doesn't really characterize the attitude toward this type of behavior in the region, except for large instances. Small examples, like inflating business expenses, are commonplace. In fact, if you ask for a receipt in a restaurant, it is not uncommon to receive a blank, stamped receipt on which you can enter whatever amount you like. Waiters are tipped generously for this service (which can of course be covered by what is put on the receipt).

WOMEN IN BUSINESS

A patriarchal, macho culture still pervades most of the business world. Even some Bosnian women show more respect for their male counterparts than their female ones. Despite this, women can be found in all kinds and levels of business, especially in the cities and in the financial industry. Men do tend to hold most management positions, and almost always make more money than their female colleagues. Some variations with ethnicity can occur as well, with Croats generally treating women in a more egalitarian manner.

Women in business are appreciated as women, and male colleagues will certainly attempt to charm them. They can be perceived as weak negotiators, so visiting businesswomen should establish a confident (but not superior!) attitude from the beginning. Charm works both ways, and a little modest flirting is not only permitted, but may also help things along.

chapter nine

COMMUNICATING

LANGUAGE

Many travelers ask what language is spoken in
Bosnia and Herzegovina. This question is
surprisingly difficult to answer. Formally, the
official language is known as Bosnian, and this was
adopted in the Bosnian Constitution in 1992 when
the country declared its independence. To be
politically correct, the language of the region is
commonly called Bosnian-Croatian-Serbian, or
BCS. While, practically, Bosnian is nearly identical
to Serbian and Croatian, the names of the languages
carry political importance. Slight differences do
exist in the case of certain words, and using one
form or another identifies one's nationality, much
as an accent might. Comparing the languages of
Bosnia and its bordering countries is like
comparing American English with British and
Australian English; people take pride in their
particular version of the language and seek to
distinguish themselves through its use.

Until the fall of Yugoslavia, one language, Serbian,
was used throughout the Balkan region. Upon its
collapse, the languages began to diverge. This

divergence was encouraged by nationalists in each country in order to establish the individuality and independence of each region. The languages continue to move apart even today as this process continues.

In Bosnia, this has become increasingly complicated. Divided as it is between the RS and the Federation, distinctions in the language are visible even within the country. The Latin alphabet is used in the Federation, while the Cyrillic alphabet is used in the RS. Even in Sarajevo, where parts of the outlying city spill into the RS, signs abruptly change to Cyrillic. While this can be confusing to those unfamiliar with Cyrillic, the alphabet is not very difficult to learn. Since the Latin alphabet is used in most of Sarajevo, travelers shouldn't have too much trouble reading signs within the city.

The language itself is extraordinarily complicated, and the grammar bears little resemblance to English grammar. Bosnian assigns one of three genders to words: male, female, or neuter. Nouns have seven different cases. Verb endings change based on whether you're talking about a location, asking a question, or requesting some sort of action. There are no definite or indefinite articles. There are formal and informal forms of address. Learning the intricacies of the language can seem overwhelming at first, but the linguistic nuances of Bosnian are truly fascinating and worth investigating.

Thankfully, BCS is a phonetic language and words are pronounced exactly as they're spelled. Most of the letters are pronounced as they are in English, with a few exceptions. The sound of the language itself is not unpleasant; it has a slightly "thicker" sound to the English ear, but has a lyricism that provides a nice balance. A few of the sounds may be difficult for English speakers to pronounce, but most Bosnians will appreciate the attempt and foreigners will be forgiven their mistakes. Most Bosnians, especially those who themselves speak other languages, are cheerfully aware of the complications of their own language, and will sympathize with visitors in their efforts.

In Sarajevo, many waiters, waitresses, and shopkeepers speak English, but most taxi drivers and bus drivers do not. If you need help, look for a young person, as many now speak at least basic English. Outside the capital few people speak English, and a good phrase book is invaluable.

Guide to Bosnian Pronunciation

c	**ts**
ć	**tch**, as the "t" in "creature"
č	**tch**, but thicker than ć, as in "match"
đ, dj, dž	all slight variations on **j**, as in "jungle"
j	**y**, as in "Yugoslavia"
lj	**lya**, as in "billion"
nj	**ny**, as in "Sonya"
r	slightly rolled, as in Spanish
š	**sh**, as in "shelter"
ž	**zh**, as in "Zhivago"

Some Basic Words and Phrases

Dobro jutro	Good morning (said until about midday)
Dobar dan	Good day (said from about midday to dusk)
Dobro veče	Good evening
Laku noć	Good night (when departing; the other three are greetings)
Kako si?	How are you?
Molim vas...	I would like . . . please (used to order food or in a shop)
Jos jedno...	One more... ("*Molim vas jos jedno pivo,*" I would like another beer, please")
Hvala	Thank you
Ne znam	I don't know
Ne razumijem	I don't understand
Da	Yes
Ne	No
Koliko košta?	How much? (cost)
Oprostite	Excuse me/I'm sorry
Ovdje	Here (to indicate the driver should stop)
Lijevo	Left
Desno	Right
Pravo	Ahead ("keep going")
Govorite li Engleski?	Do you speak English?
Ne govorim Bosanski	I don't speak Bosnian

FORMS OF ADDRESS

Hierarchy and social status are important in Bosnia, and on meeting one should use the proper, respectful form of address for "you," which is *vi*. The informal form is *ti*. Adults will use the formal *vi* until the senior person suggests relaxing the rule, although when younger people and students of the same age meet one another they will use *ti*. The formal way of addressing someone in writing is to use "*Vi*", with the first letter capitalized.

You should address individuals as "Mr." or "Mrs." followed by the exact form of their name that they give to you, so pay attention to whether they offer their first name, surname, or both. Even people you see every day, such as the shopkeeper or the waiter in your favorite café, should be addressed as "*Gospodin*" (Mr.) or "*Gospodna*" (Mrs.).

When introducing yourself, it is appropriate to offer a handshake, but men typically wait for the woman to extend her hand first. Some Muslim women do not touch men outside their family. When greeting friends, Bosnians kiss on both cheeks, but Serbs may kiss three times. Bosnians are friendly, despite all the formality of address; they make lots of eye contact, smile frequently, and actually make contact when kissing cheeks— no air kisses.

The forms of address can be complicated, but the rules begin to sort themselves out if you choose to learn the language. For the English speaker, simply observe a formal means of address unless you are asked to call them something different. Address your colleagues using "Mr." and "Mrs." from the beginning, and follow the lead of your friends as to whether or not to use their first name only.

CONVERSATION

Bosnians do not expect foreigners to speak their language, but you can win major points by using a few basic phrases. This shows respect for and interest in the country, and will receive warm responses. While young people might speak English, especially in Sarajevo, it is not guaranteed. German is commonly spoken, especially with older generations, and Italian is not uncommon.

Bosnians are curious and involved in their friends' lives. Young people like to talk about music, sports, and movies, just like youth anywhere. Although most people recommend that you avoid politics, it is a very popular topic of conversation. It's best to remain neutral and simply listen. Bosnians tend to be rather fed up with their politicians, pessimistic about political change, and feel they have no control over the political process. The American can-do spirit is not present here, and urgings to get involved politically will be met with blank stares.

The war comes up frequently, although personal stories aren't openly talked about unless you ask directly, but this can be a tricky subject. Sometimes, Bosnians will bring up the war as some sort of justification, effectively halting the conversation. You can ask for more information or let the issue rest, as the situation dictates.

Bosnians are eager to share their country with visitors, and will assume that you have no prior knowledge of its history. They often begin with the basics, which can be a little condescending to informed travelers. Don't be surprised if they begin with, "In Bosnia, we have three ethnic groups . . . " It's best just to let them talk, and respond by demonstrating your depth of understanding in order to move the conversation to a more sophisticated level.

Bosnians will be curious about you, your life back home, and why you are here. They will invariably ask where you're from, what you're doing, and if you miss your family. Even those who speak good English tend to get tripped up on translating, "How long have you been here, and when do you leave?" If they ask "How long are you here?" it's best to answer with both your arrival and departure plans, because even this seasoned traveler has yet to figure out which one they really mean.

BODY LANGUAGE
Bosnians are extremely friendly, and this is reflected in their body language. As with their Mediterranean neighbors, Bosnians express

themselves with vivid hand gestures and physical contact. In business, it is typical to greet with a handshake. Those who know each other, or in less formal situations, kiss on both cheeks. Close friends will hug, walk arm in arm, and stand very near one another. While this might be a bit disconcerting to foreigners, it is meant to be friendly.

Public affection between couples is very common, and it is not unusual to see young people kissing or sitting on laps in bars or in the parks. Men are not shy about expressing their interest in a woman on the street. If a man hollers at you, or a cabdriver calls you "*ljepa*" (pretty), don't be surprised. There is nothing wrong with returning the compliment with a smile or a thank-you. You can, of course, simply ignore it.

Body language can be quite a useful means of communication where language fails, as many Bosnian gestures are similar to American or British gestures. Connecting the forefinger and the thumb in a circle means something is especially good, and is an appropriate way of complimenting a meal or service. Throwing the right arm up and back can mean "Forget it," or can be a sign of frustration or dismissal. Obscene gestures are uncommon, but there are a few universal hand signals that are commonly understood.

SENSE OF HUMOR

Some foreigners, especially those who learn the language, may be shocked to discover the

Bosnians' dark sense of humor. In a culture where so many topics are taboo, jokes that denigrate certain ethnic groups can be quite explicit. It's best just to laugh along, rather than point out the insensitivity of the joke.

Off-color jokes are also very popular, and these may be shared even in more formal situations, like business meetings, or across generations. These jokes are often difficult to translate, as many are based on wordplay. Look out for jokes about Mujo and Haso, and their lover, Fata—these stereotypical Bosnians are the butt of many a joke. Mujo, Haso, and Fata are Muslim names, and in the jokes Fata is usually sleeping with one or the other of the men. Jokes about ethnic stereotypes are also common, and will be uttered to members of any ethnic group without pause, at least in friendly and informal situations.

SWEARING

Bosnians are a colorful lot, and swearwords will often punctuate conversations between friends. Swearing is often used to express emotion, especially when one is feeling jocular or in a particularly good mood. There are numbers of creative insults as well that involve sexual behavior or ethnic stereotypes. Foreigners who insert a carefully chosen Bosnian curse into informal conversation can create a feeling of camaraderie under the right circumstances. An American lecturer once won over a room full of college students when she accidentally swore after dropping a piece of chalk. With friends, or over drinks, you might hear swearwords used casually and non-offensively.

A GOSSIP CULTURE

Muhaluša is the Bosnian word for an old gossip, and often refers to anyone involved in others' business. By this definition, most Bosnians are *muhalušas*. To foreigners used to their privacy, the interest in and spread of personal information can be a bit of a shock. There is no such thing as a secret in Bosnia, and gossip is relished. Most Bosnians are abashedly aware of this tendency without being deterred by the implications. Foreigners should be aware of this non-malicious facet of Bosnian culture, especially in business situations. Be careful about revealing sensitive information unless you're very sure you don't mind it becoming public knowledge.

WRITING STYLE

The Bosnian mentality is reflected in their writing style, so be aware of what to expect if you ask a Bosnian to write a memo for you. Those who attended university in other parts of Europe or America will demonstrate a familiar writing style: they quickly state their purpose, provide details to support their claim, and sequence their ideas logically. Most Bosnians, however, approach written arguments in a different way. They tend to adopt a certain flow of consciousness in their writing, and it can be very florid and descriptive. Plagiarism is extremely common, and is simply viewed as a way of supporting one's argument, rather than as intellectual infringement. "If someone else has already made the point, why say it again?" seems to be the attitude. Don't let these tendencies influence your opinion about the writer's intelligence or ability; their training was simply different.

THE MEDIA

The media in Bosnia is flourishing, although most news sources are strongly partisan, therefore affecting the reliability and fairness of news availability. English-language newspapers are not commonly found, so it can be difficult to keep abreast of current events in the country during your visit.

Television

There are three main television networks that cover news, entertainment, sports, and other programs of general interest: the Radiotelevision of Bosnia–Herzegovina (BHRT), Mreza Plus, and the Open Broadcast Network. All of the

programming on these channels is in Bosnian
or Serbian; occasionally there will be English
subtitles, but not always. Federation TV (FTV) is
the public TV service for the Federation, and Serb
Republic Radio-TV (RTRS) operates in the RS.
TV Pink BH is an offshoot of a Serbian network.
In addition to the state broadcaster, it is possible
to receive some English-language channels, such
as the National Geographic Channel and the
Discovery Channel, but commercials will often
be in Bosnian. There are also German, Italian,
and Spanish channels.

Press
The Bosnian press is active and produces a great
range of local news and popular
entertainment media in the local
language. *Oslobodjenje* is a
popular paper with a
Bosniak bent. *Dnevni Avaz*
and *Nezavisne Novine*
(Serbian) are more
independent. *Dnevni List* is
produced in Mostar and therefore written in
Croatian. Major magazines are often produced in
Bosnia in the local language. Popular local
magazines include *Dani*, *Slobodna Bosna*, *Start*,
and *Most*.

Unfortunately, there are few options for
accessing local news in English. International
news companies cover major events in the region,
but not local events. *Bosnia Daily* translates the

local papers for a monthly fee, but is rather
pricey. For local events and information, the Web
site www.infobar.ba is useful.

Radio
There are four main radio stations that cover
news, entertainment, and sports. They all
operate on the FM network and have local
stations. Radio and TV of Bosnia
and Herzegovina is a statewide
channel. Radio RBiH is available
in the Federation, while Serb
Republic Radio-TV is offered in
the RS. Radio Herceg Bosna is a
Mostar-based Croat channel. There are several
other private networks that vary by region; the
language is exclusively Bosnian.

INTERNET AND E-MAIL
The use of the Internet and e-mail is growing,
although it is not as widespread as in other parts
of Europe or America. Due to economic issues,
the Internet is not ubiquitous in homes, and some
reports show that only a quarter of the population
actually uses the Internet regularly. More people
are beginning to use e-mail, but the telephone is
still the most common means of communication.
Few businesses have Web sites, and it is difficult
to find local information on the Web. Attempting
to reach business contacts via e-mail, especially

those you don't know, can be nearly impossible as most are not listed online. This can be frustrating for those who are used to relying on the Internet for information, but it is to be hoped that this will change soon.

For travelers who plan to stay in Bosnia, or who might wish to use the Internet in their friends' homes, it is wise to be aware of some of the differences in provision of service. DSL and high-speed Internet are not widespread, and slow service naturally inhibits some of the conveniences of the Internet. In addition, most providers cap a user's bandwidth and only allow a certain amount of downloads a month, usually 3MGs. Before you download that movie on your friend's computer, be aware that you might end up costing them a lot of money in excess charges. Save the big downloads for places where free Wi-Fi is available (a few cafés in Sarajevo now offer this, notably the UNITEC café). Internet cafés are very reasonably priced, but are difficult to find outside the big cities; they also tend to be dominated by boys playing video games. For travelers who set up their own Internet service, bills are usually paid at the post office.

THE POST OFFICE

The post office provides a variety of general services. In addition to mailing packages, you can pay bills, exchange money, and purchase SIM

cards there. Be sure that you
stand in the right line for
the service you need. It can
be helpful to have a Bosnian
friend with you the first time
you use the post office, as the
attendants may not speak English and are
sometimes brusque in dealing with confused
foreign customers. A package or letter mailed
from Bosnia can take one to two weeks to reach
the United States or other parts of Europe.
Shipping to Bosnia can take even longer, and
shipping packages there can be quite expensive.
It is common for Bosnians to ask international
friends to courier packages for them to mail when
they return home, but this is, of course, at your
own discretion. FedEx and DHL both offer
shipping services, but these can be extremely
pricey, if a great deal faster.

While mail sent within Bosnia is relatively
quick, you can use buses to transport packages
or documents. For a small fee, drivers will accept
parcels and drop them off along their routes.
There is no form of insurance or guarantee that
your package will get into the right hands, but
this method is commonly employed.

There are certain restrictions on what can be
mailed in Bosnia, and it is wise not to send
valuables through the post. As packages go
through customs, there is no guarantee that
jewelry or currency will arrive at its destination.

TELEPHONE

The personal cell phone is a hugely popular addition to Bosnian life, and has become something of a status symbol. Cell phones are ubiquitous in business, bars, restaurants, schools, and at home. Students tote designer phones long before they own a personal computer, and individuals don't e-mail to keep in touch, they text. Situations that require more formal means of communication in other parts of the world, like arranging a meeting, contacting a teacher, or setting up dinner plans, are accomplished via text message in Bosnia.

Even for the short-term visitor, it is wise to get a temporary cell phone while in the country. The local cell companies are BiH Telecom, Eronet, and M:TEL. You can also purchase a local SIM card at the post office or at a kiosk. International phones with GSM technology and whose carriers have a roaming agreement with Bosnia and Herzegovina will work in the country, but will be wildly expensive. It's much cheaper to rent a phone or buy a local SIM card, or simply buy a cell phone if you plan to stay for any length of time. When making calls, the dial tone is a long tone followed by a pause; the busy signal is a short tone followed by an equally short pause.

The main telephone company is PPT, but Croats and Serbs have their own companies too (HPT and

Telecom Srpski, respectively). Cell phone services are ethnically based, too; BiH Telecom is mainly used by Bosniaks, M:TEL is used by Serbs, and Eronet is used by Croats. Even though the prices and service quality vary widely between the services, people generally support the service that is associated with their ethnic group. Landline service is usually adequate, but it can be expensive with poor sound quality.

International calls can be quite expensive, and calls from hotels are especially pricey, even local calls. You can purchase phone cards at the post office or at a kiosk, but the cards are compatible only with the public telephones of the company that issued the card. The cheapest way to make international calls is to use the public telephones at the local post office. To use these, simply lift the receiver, insert the calling card, and dial the number. The card will be retuned to you after you hang up. It is wise to carry around a phone card for emergencies, as coin-operated phones don't exist.

There are other options if you wish to make long-distance phone calls. For short stays, many internationals use Skype, a free application that connects via the Internet. Many internationals who live in Bosnia use Vonage phones as well; these also use the Internet to connect and support US phone numbers, so calls to US numbers are free. Finally, callback services connect users to their home telephone grids and take advantage of local rates.

USEFUL TELEPHONE NUMBERS	
Ambulance	124
Police	122
Fire	123
Emergency roadside service	1282/1288
Emergency hospital line (Sarajevo) (English spoken)	3361-1111
Directory assistance (local)	988
Time	125

To call Bosnia from abroad, you must dial your country's access code, the Bosnian country code (387), the local prefix, and the six-digit number. There are no area codes in Bosnia, but rather prefixes that signify the location of the number or the cell phone carrier. Note that prefixes are preceded by a zero, which you drop if calling Bosnia from out of the country.

The prefix for numbers in the Federation starts with 3 (Sarajevo is 033), and numbers in the RS start with 5. Numbers in the Brcko District start with 4. Cell phone numbers start with 6 (BH telecom 61 or 62, Eronet 63, M:TEL 65).

To call a US number from Bosnia dial: 00 + 1 + US number (with area code). To call a UK number dial: 00 + 44 + number (with area code). To call Sarajevo from within Bosnia dial: 033 + 6 digit number

CONCLUSION

To visit Bosnia is to love Bosnia, but you must accept it for what it is. If you try to fight the bureaucracy and idiosyncrasies, you will not be happy here. Embrace its friendly people, relish its beautiful countryside, explore its complicated past, indulge in its laid-back lifestyle, and you will find that Bosnia gets under your skin and stays there. There is a legend that all who drink from the fountain in Bascarija will one day return; after your visit to Bosnia, hopefully you will see this as a blessing.

Insofar as current events are concerned, Bosnia is quite a safe place to visit. This does not mean that it is stable, however. As Croatia moves toward the EU and Serbia struggles to define its nationhood, Bosnia continues to be caught in the middle. The recent independence of Kosovo and the arrest of Mladić stirred up sleeping tensions. Allegiances to external identities are still present within the country, and the choices that its neighbors make will affect the direction that Bosnia follows. The future is not clear, but it is certain that big events are on the horizon. Understanding the country today will help make sense of events to come.

Although you might be frustrated by the bureaucracy, or disheartened by the hardships your local friends face, it is important to see the opportunity in BiH. Here, a substantial Muslim population peacefully coexists with Western political practices. In Sarajevo, a mosque, a synagogue, and a cathedral are all within view

of one another—and despite what you might read, the inhabitants of each want nothing more than to live peacefully with their neighbors. With rich natural resources and huge potential for ecotourism, Bosnia could theoretically do very well for itself.

But for the casual visitor, the turmoil of Bosnian politics and economics can be easily forgotten in the company of new friends. On a day-to-day basis, there is much to enjoy, from the hearty food and strong liquor, to the warmth and openness of its people, to the beautiful countryside that defines much of what is Bosnia. The people may have a degree of pessimism about their future, but they do not take kindly to being called Third World. Be careful not to peg Bosnia too quickly as a backwater—there is a way of getting things done if you are open to learning how.

That there are hardships here is undeniable. But the relaxed pace of life, the friendliness of its

people, and the beauty of the country are what
define daily life. The visitor might be inclined to
focus on the differences between Bosnia and
their home country, and some visitors focus
unnecessarily on the difficulties of life here. The
best way to enjoy Bosnia is to focus instead on
the daily pleasures of a cup of *Bosanska kafa*
with a good friend, to appreciate having the time
for personal relationships, and to respect the grit
and determination of the Bosnian people simply
to keep going forward. *Sretan put!*

Further Reading

Andrić, Ivo. *The Bridge Over the Drina*. London: The Harvill Press, 1994.

Bose, Sumantra. *Bosnia After Dayton: Nationalist Partition and International Intervention*. New York: Oxford University Press, 2002.

Clancy, Tim. *Bosnia & Herzegovina: The Bradt Travel Guide*. Chalfont St. Peter, UK: Bradt Travel Guides Ltd, 2004.

Filipović, Zlata. *Zlata's Diary: A Child's Life in Sarajevo*. New York: Viking Press, 1994.

Haviv, Ron. *Blood and Honey: A Balkan War Journal*. New York: TV Books, 2000.

The International Women's Club. *Opening Doors: A Selected Guide to Living in Sarajevo*. Tuzla: Grafičko-Izdavačka Kuća d.oo, 2006.

Lloyd, Alexander. *My War Gone By, I Miss it So*. London: Anchor Books, 2000.

Malcolm, Noel. *Bosnia: A Short History*. London: Pan Books, 2002.

Matvejević, Predrag, and Tom Stoddart. *Sarajevo*. Washington, DC: Smithsonian Institution Press, 1998.

Oliver, Ian. *War & Peace in the Balkans: The Diplomacy of Conflict in the Former Yugoslavia*. London: I.B. Tauris, 2005.

Selimović, Meša. *Death and Dervish*. Evanston, IL: Northwestern University Press, 1996.

Thomas, Raju G.C., ed. *Yugoslavia Unraveled: Sovereignty, Self-Determination, Intervention*. Lanham, MD: Lexington Books, 2003.

culture smart! **bosnia and herzegovina**

Index

Acknowledgments

I have drawn upon the works of Tim Clancy and Noel Malcolm
(see Further Reading) for much of the history section of this book.

I would like to thank all of the lifelong friends I've made during my time
in Bosnia for sharing their incredible country with me: Branka, Ramajana,
Dzana, Mirzana, Maja, Irma, Damir, Azra, Emira, Dzenana, Emir, Ajla,
Lillit, Lejla, and, especially, my students. Finally, to Matt, for his
unflagging and indispensable support and encouragement—here's to
the hadrons, because they matter.